ESSENTIALS
OF PARTNERSHIP
TAXATION

PAUL R. ERICKSON, JD, CPA

Associate Professor of Taxation
Baylor University

Library of Congress Cataloging-in-Publication Data

Erickson, Paul R., 1946-
  Essentials of partnership taxation.

  1. Partnership—Taxation—United States. I. Title.
  KF6452.E75   1989   343.7306'62   89-3535
  ISBN 0-13-286717-6   347.303662

Editorial/production supervision and
  interior design: Anthony Calcara
Cover design: 20/20 Services, Inc.
Manufacturing buyer: Ed O'Dougherty

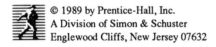

Printed in the United States of America

10 9 8 7 6 5 4 3 2 1

ISBN 0-13-286717-6

PRENTICE-HALL INTERNATIONAL (UK) LIMITED, *London*
PRENTICE-HALL OF AUSTRALIA PTY. LIMITED, *Sydney*
PRENTICE-HALL CANADA INC., *Toronto*
PRENTICE-HALL HISPANOAMERICANA, S.A., *Mexico*
PRENTICE-HALL OF INDIA PRIVATE LIMITED, *New Delhi*
PRENTICE-HALL OF JAPAN, INC., *Tokyo*
SIMON & SCHUSTER ASIA PTE. LTD., *Singapore*
EDITORA PRENTICE-HALL DO BRASIL, LTDA., *Rio de Janeiro*

TABLE OF CONTENTS

PREFACE

Essentials of Partnership Taxation is the perfect supplement for both basic and advanced courses on Partnership Taxation. It is designed to be used with Master's level courses in accounting as well as law school courses. It may be used in professional continuing education courses or in-house training programs sponsored by legal or accounting firms. It may also be used as an aid to self-study for those individuals who desire in-depth knowledge in the area of partnership taxation.

This book provides a detailed outline of the tax law as it applies to partnerships and partners. It organizes the many rules contained in the Code, Registration, Cases, and Revenue Rulings into logical areas such as formation, operations, distributions, liquidations, etc. Included are numerous questions and problems together with answers. The questions and problems are designed to provide an opportunity to the student to self-test his or her knowledge in particular areas. Many of the questions are thought-provoking, which allow the student to improve analytical skills.

This book is most helpful when used in conjunction with other materials, such as one of the two major treatises on partnership taxation, law casebooks, college textbooks or continuing education materials. In order to aid the interaction between this book and the above mentioned works, a textbook-treatise correlation chart is included.

This book contains rules of law which are current through November 15, 1988, which includes the Technical and Miscellaneous Revenue Act of 1988, as well as any regulations, rulings and case decisions issued thereto.

Partnership Taxation Textbook Correlation Chart

Erickson Parts	Lind Chapters	McKee Chapters	Strueling Pages	Willis Chapters
I	1	3	13-24,416-425	2,3,184
IIA	2A,2B	4	40-43	22-24,44
IIB	2C,2D	5	43-59	26,27
III	2B.1,3A.2	6 & 7	59-63,149-170	31-33,41-46
IV	3A.1	9	89-96,170-179	71-73
V	3B	10.1-10.9	97-132	25,81-87
VI	3A.3	10.10	132-139	51-64
VII	3D	14	432-442	171-175
VIII	6D.2	11 & 12	Ch.7	74,131-133
IX	3C	13	179-193	91-97
X	4	15	244-259	42,101
XI	4A,5D	16	319-328	102
XII	5A-5C	19 & 20	Ch.5	111-114,154 ,156
XIII	5D	21	332-362	121-123
XIV	6 & 7	22 & 23	260-283	141-148,151, 152,155
XV	4B,5B,5C	24 - 26	Ch.9	34,103,104, 115,153

LIND, SCHWARTZ, LATHROPE, AND ROSENBERG; *Fundamentals of Partnership Taxation*, Foundation Press, 1985

MCKEE, NELSON, AND WHITMIRE; *Federal Taxation of Partnerships and Partners*, Warren, Gorham and Lamont, 1987

STREULING, BOYD AND HELLER; *Federal Taxation of Partners and Partnerships*, Prentice Hall, 1986

WILLIS, PENNELL AND POSTLEWAITE; *Partnership Taxation*, Shepard's/McGraw Hill, 1987

I.

WHAT CONSTITUTES
A PARTNERSHIP

A. STATUTORY DEFINITIONS

1. **Uniform Partnership Act:** Section 6 provides in part
   a. A partnership is an association of two or more persons to carry on as co-owners a business for a profit.
   b. "But any association formed under any other statute of this state...is not a partnership under this act...but this act shall apply to limited partnerships..."
2. **Internal Revenue Code:** Code sections 761(a) and 7701(a)(2), and regulation 1.761-1(a) can be separated into two important elements.
   a. Some combination of taxpayers for conducting business,
   b. which is not a corporation, trust, or estate.
3. **Difference:** The important difference between the two is profit motive.
4. **Controlling Law:** Federal law supersedes state law in determining the existence of a partnership for tax purposes. [Reg 301.7701-1(b) and *Commissioner v Tower*, 327 US 280 (1946)]

B. CASE LAW DEFINITIONS

1. **Objective Test:** In *Commissioner v Tower* (supra) the Court identified a number of objective factors for determining whether a partnership existed or not.

2. **Subjective Test:** In *Culbertson v Commissioner*, 337 US 733 (1949), the Court overruled the *Tower* case saying that status is based on "intent" after considering all the "facts and circumstances."

C. ELECTION OUT

1. **Rule:** An organization that qualifies as a partnership under Subchapter K can elect not to be taxed as a partnership if it falls into one of the following categories. [Sec 761(a)]
   a. Investment purposes only
   b. Joint production, extraction, or use of property
   c. Certain security transactions by dealers
2. **Requirements:** Specific requirements must be met in order to qualify for the election. [See Reg 1.761-2]

D. OTHER ARRANGEMENTS

1. **Employer–Employee:** An arrangement where one individual owned all the assets and another individual received a percent of the profits was held to be an employment relationship rather than a partnership. [*Estate of Kahn v Commissioner*, 499 F2d 1186 (2d Cir 1974)]
2. **Lender–Borrower**
   a. An advance of funds for purchase and development of property followed by a distribution of developed property to the party making the advance was held not to be a joint venture, but rather compensation for financial services. [*Ian T. Allison*, 35 TCM 1069 (1976)]
   b. Advance of funds to a local unit of government to build a ferry, followed by repayment of original funds plus interest and then a profit sharing arrangement, was held to be a partnership from the outset. [*Eugene C. Hartman*, 17 TCM 1020 (1958)]
3. **Co-ownership:** Mere joint ownership of property does not constitute a partnership. [Reg 1.761-1(a)]
   a. Renting, leasing, or providing customary services does not change the result.
   b. Providing noncustomary services through an agent who retains the entire proceeds therefrom does not constitute a partnership. [Rev Rul 75-374, 1975-2 CB 261]
4. **Expense Sharing:** Mere sharing of expenses without sharing profits from a joint undertaking does not constitute a partnership. [Reg 1.761-1(a)]
5. **In-Kind Profits:** Sharing the expense of constructing a power plant followed by each participant taking its share of power and selling such separately did

constitute a partnership. [*Madison Gas and Electric Company*, 72 TC 521 (1979), aff'd, 633 F2d 512 (7th Cir 1980)]

6. **Substance over Form**

   a. Characterization of a joint venture as a corporate transaction through issuance and redemption of preferred stock in order to obtain capital gain treatment was held to be a partnership. [*S & M Plumbing Co*, 55 TC 702 (1971)]

   b. Formation of a corporation merely to obtain financing for a partnership, where state law prevented the partnership from obtaining the loan due to usury law, did result in the organization being recharacterized as a corporation. [*Roccaforte*, 77 TC 263 (1981), revd, 708 F2d 986 (5th Cir 1983); Rev Rul 75-31, 1975-1 CB 10 and Rev Rul 76-26, 1976-1 CB 10]

E. ASSOCIATION STATUS

1. **Result:** Any partnership with more corporate characteristics than partnership characteristics will be treated as a corporation for tax purposes. [Reg 301.7701-2]

2. **Critical Characteristics:** Although six characteristics are listed, only the following four are used in the test, which means that any partnership possessing three of the four will be taxed as a corporation.

   a. **Continuity of life:** When death, insanity, bankruptcy, retirement, resignation, or expulsion of any member will not cause a dissolution of the organization. [Reg 301.7701-2(b)(1)]

   b. **Centralized management:** Exclusive authority, held by any one person or group of less than all members, to make management decisions necessary to conduct the business of the organization. [Reg 301.7701-2(c)(1)]

   c. **Limited liability:** Where no member of the organization is personally liable for debts of the organization under local law. [Reg 301.7701-2(d)(1)]

   d. **Free transferability of interests:** The power of each member to transfer his ownership in the organization to a non-member without the consent of the other members. [Reg 301.7701-2(e)(1)]

3. **Partnerships Affected:** Due to the legal requirements of a general partnership, only limited partnerships need to be concerned with the "association" problem.

4. **Easy Out:** Compliance with the Uniform Limited Partnership Act provisions results in taxation as a partnership. [Reg 301.7701-2]

   a. **Caution:** Some states' versions do not qualify.

   b. **Check:** The Internal Revenue Service periodically publishes a list of those states whose provisions qualify.

II.

PARTNERSHIP FORMATION

A. PROPERTY CONTRIBUTIONS

1. **Tax Free:** Gain or loss is recognized by neither the partnership nor any partner upon contribution of property to the partnership in exchange for an interest therein. [Sec 721(a)]

   a. **Property** includes money, real and personal property, tangible and intangible property, but does not include services. [Reg 1.721-1(b)]

   b. **Effect of liabilities**

      1) **Increase** in a partner's share of partnership liabilities is treated as a contribution of money by such partner. [Sec 752(a)]

      2) **Decrease** in a partner's share of partnership liabilities is treated as a distribution of money to such partner. [Sec 752(b)]

   c. **Exceptions to nonrecognition of gain**

      1) **Investment company** contributions. [Sec 721(b)]

      2) **Liabilities exceeding basis:** Partnership assumption of a contributing partner's liabilities that exceed the basis of his partnership interest results in a taxable distribution. [Sec 731(a)(1) in conjunction with Sec 752(b)]

      3) **Example:** A, B, and C form an equal partnership. A and B each contribute $20,000 cash. C contributes property worth $50,000, with a basis to C of $15,000. The property is encumbered by a $30,000 mortgage, which the partnership assumes. Since C is relieved of

4

$20,000 worth of liabilities on the contribution, she must recognize a $5000 gain, the portion of the liabilities (applicable to A and B) in excess of her basis.

2. Contributing Partner's Basis in Partnership

a. Definition

1) **Official:** Exchanged basis. [Sec 7701(a)(44)]

2) **Common:** Often referred to as "outside" basis.

b. Rule: Basis the partner had in the contributed property immediately prior to contribution, plus any money he contributed, plus any gain recognized under section 721(b). [Sec 722]

c. Holding Period: The contributing partner may tack the holding period of contributed property to the holding period of her partnership interest if at the time of contribution the property contributed was a capital asset or asset used in her trade or business. [Sec 1223(1)]

d. Example: M contributes to the ML partnership equipment worth $10,000 with a basis of $7000. M also contributes $5000 cash. L contributes land worth $25,000 with a basis of $20,000 and encumbered by a mortgage of $10,000, which is assumed by the partnership. M and L both have a 50% interest in the partnership. M's basis for his interest is $17,000 (basis in equipment plus cash and share of partnership liabilities). L's basis for his interest is $15,000 (basis in land less liabilities assumed by the partnership plus share of partnership liabilities).

3. Partnership's Basis in Contributed Property

a. Definition

1) **Official:** Transferred basis. [Sec 7701(a)(43)]

2) **Common:** Often referred to as "inside" basis

b. Rule: Basis the contributing partner had in the property immediately prior to contribution, plus any gain recognized by the contributing partner under section 721(b). [Sec 723]

c. Holding Period: A partnership always tacks the partner's prior holding period to its own holding period of the contributed assets. [Sec 1223(2)]

d. Example: In the ML partnership example above, the partnership has a $7000 basis in the equipment and a $20,000 basis in the land.

4. Recapture

a. Depreciation: Potential recapture under sections 1245 and 1250 carries over to the partnership. [Regs 1.1245-2(c)(2) and 1.1250-3(c)(3)]

b. Investment tax credit: Potential recapture on contributed property carries over to the partnership. However, upon early disposition of the asset, the contributing partner must recognize the recapture. [Sec 47]

5. Cash Basis Accounts Receivable

    a. Assignment of income

        1) Subchapter C: Transfer of accounts receivable from a cash basis tax-payer to an accrual basis corporation is not an assignment of income. [*Hempt Bros. v United States*, 490 F2d 1172 (3d Cir 1974) and Rev Rul 80-198, 1980-2 CB 113]

        2) Subchapter K: While there is no similar provision for partnerships the principles of Subchapter C should be applicable.

    b. Allocation of income: Income from cash basis receivables contributed after 3-31-84 must be allocated to the contributing partner when collected by the partnership. [Sec 704(c)]

6. Cash Basis Accounts Payable

    a. Liabilities ???

        1) Subchapter C: Accounts payable transferred to an accrual basis cor-poration, where the amount of such payables exceeds the basis of property transferred, are not considered liabilities for the purpose of determining gain on the transfer. [Sec 357(c) and *Donald D. Focht*, 68 TC 223 (1977)]

        2) Subchapter K

            a) The Conference Committee stated that Rev. Rul. 60-345 should not be followed and that accrued but unpaid items should not be treated as partnership liabilities for section 752 purposes. [H Rep No 98-861, 98th Cong, 2d Sess (1984)]

            b) In Rev. Rul. 88-77 (1988-38 IRB 8), the Service revoked Rev. Rul. 60-345, holding that accrued liabilities of the *partnership* do not con-stitute basis adjustments for purposes of section 752.

    b. Expense allocation: For liabilities contributed after 3-31-84, the expense must be allocated to the contributing partner when paid by the partnership. [Sec 704(c)]

7. Unrealized Precontribution Gain or Loss

    a. Allocation

        1) Rule: Any gain or loss not recognized prior to contribution must be al-located to the contributing partner upon recognition by the partnership. [Sec 704(c)]

        2) Example: Partner S contributes to a partnership land worth $50,000 with a basis of $10,000. Later the partnership sells the land for $80,000 resulting in a $70,000 taxable gain. The first $40,000 of gain must be allocated to S. The remaining $30,000 will be shared according to the partnership agreement.

    b. Character of gain or loss on subsequent partnership dispositions of con-tributed inventory, unrealized receivables, or capital loss property is the same as it would have been to the contributing partner. [Sec 724]

8. **Sale versus Contribution**
   a. A contribution of property to a partnership followed by a distribution to the same partner within a relatively short period of time may constitute a disguised sale of such property to the partnership. [Sec 707(a)(2)(B)]
   b. See *John H. Otey*, 70 TC 312 (1978), affd per curiam, 634 F2d 1046 (6th Cir 1980); where facts similar to the above did not result in a sale.

B. SERVICE CONTRIBUTIONS

1. **Taxation of Partner:** Performance of services in exchange for property results in gross income to the one providing services. [Sec 83(a)]
   a. **Property:** Since an interest in a partnership constitutes property (a capital asset under section 1221), the exchange of services for an interest in a partnership constitutes a taxable event.
   b. **Nonrecognition:** The tax-free exchange provisions of section 721(a) apply only to contributions of property in exchange for a partnership interest. [Reg 1.721-1(b)(1) and *Sol Diamond*, 56 TC 530 (1971), affd 492 F2d 286 (7th Cir 1974)]
   c. **Capital interest:** If any partners give up their rights to repayment of contributed capital in exchange for services, the partner providing the services recognizes income. [Reg 1.721-1(b)(1) and *United States v Frazell*, 213 F 335 F2d 487 (5th Cir 1964)]
   d. **Profit interest:** Services exchanged for a partnership interest in profits is a taxable event [*Sol Diamond*], but may result in no measurable income as discussed below.
2. **Amount Included:** The partner who performs the services must include in gross income the fair market value of the partnership interest received in exchange for the services provided. [Sec 83(a)]
   a. **Capital interest**
      1) **Rule:** The service partner includes the fair market value of the capital relinquished by the other partners. [Reg 1.721-1(b)(1)]
      2) **Example:** The equal AB partnership admits C as an equal one-third partner in exchange for services provided to the partnership. C is credited with $20,000 in capital, one-third of the total capital before admission. C must recognize $20,000 in ordinary income.
   b. **Profit interest:** The service partner includes the fair market value of the partnership interest received. [Sec 83(a)]
      1) **Past services:** Measured by the value of the services provided, determined by the selling price of the partnership interest three weeks subsequent to acquisition. [*Sol Diamond*]

     2) **Future services**

       a) **Speculative:** Value was too speculative to determine. [*St. John vs United States*, 84-1 USTC #9158 (CD Ill. 1983)]

       b) **Worthless** value [*Kenroy, Inc. vs Commissioner*, 47 TCM 1749 (1984)]

3. Date Included

  a. Generally: When the interest becomes

   1) **transferable**

   OR

   2) **nonforfeitable.** [Sec 83(a)]

  b. Election: The taxpayer may elect to include the fair market value of a restricted interest in gross income. [Sec 83(b)]

   1) **Benefit:** Conversion of potential ordinary income to capital gains. (Due to repeal of the long-term capital gain deduction by the 1986 Tax Reform Act the benefit is minimal.)

   2) **Detriment**

    a) **Rule:** Any loss attributable to a basis increase as a result of the election is not allowed if the interest is later forfeited. [Reg 1.83-2(a)]

    b) **Example:** Partner D receives a restricted partnership interest in profits only in exchange for services previously provided to a partnership. The interest is worth $10,000. D makes the election under section 83(b) and recognizes $10,000 in income, and as a result has a $10,000 basis in her partnership interest. D later makes a $5000 cash contribution to the partnership, thus increasing her basis to $15,000. D subsequently forfeits her entire interest in the partnership. D is allowed to claim only a $5000 loss. The amount attributable to the section 83(b) election is disallowed.

4. Treatment to Partnership

  a. Gain recognition

   1) **Rule:** The partnership recognizes gain to the extent the interest exchanged for services is partially or wholly represented by appreciated property. [Reg 1.83-6(b)]

   2) **Example:** The equal XY partnership owns property with a fair market value of $90,000 and basis of $30,000. Z is admitted as an equal one-third partner in exchange for performing services for the partnership. The partnership has engaged in a taxable exchange and recognizes $20,000 in gain (appreciation on the one-third interest received by Z).

  b. Deduction: The partnership is entitled to deduct currently or capitalize (whichever is appropriate) an amount equal to the amount recognized as income by the partner contributing services. [Reg 1.83-6(a)(1)]

   1) **Allocation:** Although the deduction can be allocated in any manner the partners choose (see Part V), it should be allocated to those

partners who relinquish capital to the partner contributing the services.

2) **Example:** The equal AB partnership admits C as an equal one-third partner in exchange for services provided to the partnership. C is credited with $20,000 in capital, one-third of the total capital before admission. A's capital account is reduced by $15,000 and B's capital account is reduced by $5000. C is required to recognize $20,000 in ordinary income and the partnership is entitled to a $20,000 deduction. The deduction should be allocated $15,000 to A and $5000 to B.

C. ORGANIZATION COSTS

1. **Definition:** Those which are
   a. incident to the creation of the partnership,
   b. chargeable to the capital account, and
   c. beneficial to the partnership throughout its life; but which are not syndication expenses, i.e., those connected with the issuing and marketing of partnership interests. [Reg 1.709-2]
2. **General rule:** No deduction [Sec 709(a)]
3. **Election:** The partnership may elect to amortize organization expenses over a period of not less than 60 months, beginning with the month in which the partnership begins business. [Sec 709(b)(1)]

III.

PARTNERSHIP INTEREST BASIS

A. IMPORTANCE

1. **Gain or Loss:** Used for determining gain or loss on sale or exchange of a partner's partnership interest.
2. **Limitation:** Sets the limit for the amount of loss that can be passed through to the partner. [See discussion under loss limitation in Part VI]

B. CALCULATION

1. **Starting point** is the partner's basis derived from contribution of property to the partnership under section 722; or the basis derived from some other transaction under section 742, which is simply basis derived under the rules of Subchapter O (e.g., cost when purchased or fair market value when inherited). [Sec 705(a)]
2. **Increases:** Sum of partner's distributive share of
   a. taxable income,
   b. tax exempt income, and
   c. excess depletion deductions (over the basis of property being depleted. [Sec 705(a)(1)]
3. **Decreases:** Sum of
   a. distributions to the partner,
   b. partner's distributive share of losses,

    c. partner's distributive share of nondeductible expenses, and

    d. partner's distributive share of depletion (to the extent of the depleted property's basis). [Sec 705 (a)(2) & (3)]

4. Limitation: Basis in a partnership interest may never be reduced below zero. [Sec 705(a)(2)]

5. Effect of Liabilities

    a. Increase: Since an increase in a partner's share of partnership liabilities is treated as a contribution of money under section 752(a), the partner will receive a corresponding increase in basis under section 722.

    b. Decrease: Likewise, a reduction in a partner's share of partnership liabilities is treated as a distribution of money under section 752(b) and results in basis decrease under section 705(a)(2).

    c. Recourse debt is shared among the partners according to their ratio for sharing losses. [Reg 1.752-1(e)]

    d. Nonrecourse debt is shared among the partners according to their ratio for sharing profits. [Reg 1.752-1(e)]

    e. Classification of liabilities is often subject to abuse and there has been substantial clarification in this area.

        1) Accrued expenses of the partnership are not liabilities for basis adjustment purposes. [Rev Rul 88-77, 1988-38 IRB 8]

        2) Contingent liabilities did not increase basis since no liability had been fixed. [*Albany Car Wheel Co.*, 40 TC 831 (1983)]

        3) Inflated nonrecourse debt incurred for the purpose of increasing basis constitutes a sham and will be disallowed in computing basis. [Rev Rul 81-278, 1981-2 CB 159 and *Estate of Franklin*, 64 TC 752 (1975); aff'd, 544 F2d 1045 (9th Cir 1976)]

        4) Subsequent transfer of nonrecourse debt converted such to recourse debt under Washington state law. [*Richard C. Brown*, 40 TCM 725 (1980)]

        5) Guaranty of nonrecourse debt by general partner converted such to recourse debt. [*Raphan*, 759 F2d 879 (Fed Cir 1985), reversing 3 Cls Ct 457 (1983). Accord Rev Rul 83-151, 1983-2 CB 105]

        6) Nonrecourse loan by a general partner to the limited partners, followed by a contribution to the partnership by the limited partners, is a contribution to capital of the partnership by the general partner. [Rev Rul 72-135, 1972-1 CB 200]

        7) Guarantee by limited partner directly to general partner does not constitute liability to the partnership. [Rev Rul 69-223, 1969-1 CB 184]

        8) Guaranty of recourse debt to creditors (rather than to the partnership) by the limited partners should not convert the liability to recourse debt for the purpose of providing basis to limited partners. [Reg 1.752-1(e), Rev Rul 69-223 (supra), and *Richard C. Brown* (supra)]

9) **Partially recourse and partially nonrecourse** debt must be bifurcated into separate parts for purposes of section 752. [Rev Rul 84-118, 1984-2 CB 120]

10) **Planning caveat (flips or flip-flops):** In limited partnerships, it is common for the limited partners to have a larger share of losses and subsequent profits in the early years. At the point in time that the limited partners recover their investment, their profit/loss ratio is reduced. The reduction may cause a hypothetical distribution under section 752(b) which exceeds basis, resulting in gain recognition by the limited partners.

11) **Fair market value:** For purposes of section 752, debt assumed by the partnership on contributed property is limited to the fair market value of the property on which the debt is assumed. [Sec 752(c) & dictum from *Tufts*, 70 TC 756 (1978), revd, 651 F2d 1058 (5th Cir 1981) revd, 461 US 300 (1983)] ·

C. ALTERNATIVE BASIS RULE

1. **Regulations:** The Secretary of the Treasury has the power to prescribe regulations for determining basis under an alternative rule based on partners' shares of partnership asset basis. [Sec 705(b)]

2. **Rule:** A partner's basis may be determined by reference to his proportionate share of partnership asset basis that would be distributable to him upon liquidation. [Reg 1.705-1(b)]

   a. This method may only be used when the general rule of section 705(a) cannot be applied and the result will not vary from that determined under section 705(a).

   b. Any adjustments that would have been reflected in the calculation under section 705(a) must be made.

   c. Under the simplest of situations the amount will be equal to the partner's capital account plus share of partnership liabilities.

IV.

PARTNERSHIP TAX LIABILITY

A. DETERMINATION OF TAX LIABILITY

1. **Conduit:** Income and loss are passed through to the partners, who are taxed on their respective share. The partnership does not pay income tax. [Sec 701]
2. **Partnership Computations**
   a. **Same as individual.** [Sec 703(a)]
   b. **Exceptions**
      1) **Separately stated items** include short and long term capital gains and losses, section 1231 gains and losses, charitable contributions, dividends qualifying for the dividend exclusion, taxes, or any other item prescribed in the Regulations. [Reg 1.702(a)(1)-(7)]
         a) The separately stated requirement exists because of the varying treatment the items may receive when reported by the different partners on their individual tax returns.
         b) Any income or expense not required to be stated separately constitutes partnership "taxable income." [Sec 702(a)(8)]
         c) Because of an amendment to the Code without a corresponding change in the Regulations, the enumeration of separately stated items is not parallel.
      2) **Deductions not allowed** to a partnership include those for personal exemptions, foreign taxes paid, charitable contributions, net operating losses, excess itemized deductions, and depletion on oil and gas wells. [Sec 703(a)(2)]

3. **Character Determination:** Gains, losses, income, deductions, and credits are determined at the partnership level, and the character of such items flows through to the partners. [Sec 702(b)]

4. **Elections:** Any election affecting the computation of taxable income derived from the partnership must be made at the partnership level. [Sec 703(b)]

   a. See section 703(b) for exceptions.

   b. Failure to make elections by the partnership preclude the individual partners from taking advantage of such elections.

5. **Tax Return** requirements for the partnership:

   a. **Form 1065:** The partnership files an information return only, due on or before the 15th day of the fourth month following the close of the partnership's taxable year. [Sec 6072(a)]

   b. **Schedule K-1:** The partnership must furnish each partner with a schedule K-1 which summarizes their respective shares of partnership items.

   c. **Failure to comply** with filing requirements can result in a $50 per partner per month penalty for a maximum of five months. [Sec 6698]

B. PARTNERSHIP TAXABLE YEAR

1. The partnership may not have a taxable year different from that of its majority partner(s). [Sec 706(b)(1)(B)(i)]

2. If a majority of the partners are not using the same taxable year, the partnership must use a calendar year unless approval to adopt a fiscal year for a business purpose is granted by the Commissioner. [Sec 706 (b)(1)(C)]

C. PARTNERS' DISTRIBUTIVE SHARE

1. Distributive share is determined according to the partnership agreement. [Sec 704(a)]

2. Partners must report their share, whether actually distributed or not. [Reg 1.702-1(a)]

3. See Part V.

V.

PARTNERSHIP ALLOCATIONS

A. DETERMINING EACH PARTNER'S SHARE

1. **Agreement:** The determination of each partner's share of income, loss, and all other partnership items is made according to the partnership agreement. [Sec 704(a)]

   a. **Flexibility:** As long as the sharing arrangements have substantial economic effect, the partners may share any item in any ratio they choose.

   b. **Modification:** The partnership agreement includes any modifications made up to the time for filing the partnership tax return, excluding extensions. [Sec 761(c)]

2. **Nonexistent or Invalid Agreement:** The partners must share items according to their interests in the partnership. [Sec 704(b)]

3. **Partners' Interests in Partnership**

   a. **Factors:**

      1) relative contributions,

      2) share of economic profits and losses,

      3) share of cash flow and other nonliquidating distributions, and

      4) rights to distributions of capital upon liquidation. [Reg 1.704-1(b)(3)(ii)]

   b. **Presumption:** There is a rebuttable presumption that all partners' interests are equal. [Reg 1.704-1(b)(3)(i)]

4. Contributed Property

   a. Precontribution differences: Any amount of income, deduction, gain, or loss must be shared by taking into account the contributing partners' varying interests between basis and fair market value at the time of contribution. [Sec 704(c)]

     1) Example: A and B form a partnership and agree to share profits 50:50. A contributes land with a basis of $2,000 and fair market value of $10,000. B contributes $10,000 cash. Later, the partnership sells the land for $11,000. $8,000 of the $9,000 gain, attributable to precontribution appreciation, must be allocated to A. The remaining $1,000 gain is split equally between A and B.

   b. Ceiling rule: Depreciation, depletion, gain, or loss cannot be allocated in a manner which causes one or more partners to recognize more than was actually realized by the partnership. [Reg 1.704-1(c)(2)(i)]

     1) Example: A and B are equal partners in the AB partnership. The partnership admits C at a time when securities with a basis of $6,000 are worth $12,000. Subsequent to C's entry the securities are sold at a $3,000 gain ($3,000 market value decline subsequent to C's entry). The partners may not allocate $3,000 gain to both A and B, followed by a $1,000 loss allocation to all three. There was only gain recognized and no loss was realized. [Rev Rul 75-458, 1975-2 CB 258]

B. SUBSTANTIAL ECONOMIC EFFECT

1. Underlying Concept: Tax treatment should parallel economic reality.

2. Dual Test: Compliance with the tests below provides a safe harbor for special allocations.

   a. Economic effect:

     1) Capital account maintenance: An allocation will have economic effect if the partnership agreement requires that

       a) the allocation is reflected in the partner's capital account,

       b) liquidating distributions are required to be made in accordance with positive capital account balances,
       AND

       c) all partners are unconditionally required (by agreement or state law) to restore any deficit balance in their capital account upon liquidation. [Reg 1.704-1(b)(2)(ii)(b)]

     2) Economic equivalence: Even if the above are not met, an allocation will be deemed to have economic effect if actual results produce the same results as the capital account maintenance requirements. [Reg 1.704-1(b)(2)(i)]

b. Substantiality: An allocation is substantial if there is a reasonable possibility it will substantially affect the dollar amounts to be received by the partners, independent of tax consequences. [Reg 1.704-1(b)(2)(iii)]

   1) **Overall effect:** If one or more partners' after-tax position is enhanced, one or more partners' after-tax position must be correspondingly diminished.

   2) **Specific tests:** An allocation will not be substantial if at the time of the allocation there is a strong likelihood that tax consequences are

     a) **Shifting:** The shift in tax consequences disproportionately outweighs the shift in economic consequences [Reg 1.704-1(b)(2)(iii)(b)]
     OR

     b) **Transitory:** The economic effect is merely transitory due to subsequent offsetting allocations made within five years of the original allocations. [Reg 1.704-1(b)(2)(iii)(c)]

   3) **Gain charge-backs**

     a) **Definition:** Subsequent gains allocated to a partner who was previously allocated losses on the same property (usually, but not necessarily in equal amounts).

     b) **Status:** Charge-backs along with the original allocations have substantial economic effect if there is not a substantial likelihood that the allocations are merely transitory.

     c) **Example:** Partner X is allocated all depreciation expense on an office building. Upon sale of the building, gain equal to the prior depreciation deductions is first to be allocated to X with any additional gain allocated equally among all the partners. The allocations are not merely transitory if at the time the depreciation allocations were made, there was no guarantee the building could later be sold at a gain sufficient to substantially offset the prior deductions.

3. Noncompliance: Failure to comply with either the substantial economic effect test or the special rules of Reg 1.704-1(b)(4) will result in partnership items being allocated according to the partners' interests in the partnership.

4. Property Revaluations

  a. Mandatory: For the first taxable year beginning after April 30, 1986, all partnerships must revalue capital accounts to reflect fair market value of partnership assets. [Reg 1.704-1(b)(2)(iv)(r)]

  b. Elective: Upon contribution or distribution of property for a partnership interest, the partnership may elect to revalue capital accounts at the time of such transaction. [Reg 1.704-1(b)(2)(iv)(f)]

c. **Accounting:** The regulations contain numerous rules regarding account-ing treatment for disparities between book values and tax bases. [Reg 1.704-1(b)(2)(iv)]

C. RETROACTIVE ALLOCATIONS

1. **Past Abuse:** Allocating a substantial amount of the year's losses (or expen-ses) to a limited partner in a high tax bracket, who joins the partnership late in the tax year.

2. **Solution:** If during any taxable year a partner's interest changes, then each partners' distributive share of income, gain, loss, deduction, or credit is determined by taking into account the varying interests of the partners during the taxable year. [Sec 706(d)(1)]

   a. **Example:** The AB partnership admits C as an equal partner on July 1. The partnership sustains a $12,000 loss for the year. C's share of the loss is $2,000 (1/3 of 1/2 of $12,000). A and B may share the remaining $10,000 according to their partnership agreement.

   b. **Regulations:** The Secretary is to prescribe by regulations the methods to be used in determining the varying interest of the partners. [Sec 706(d)(1)]

   c. **Cash basis items** must be prorated on a day-to-day basis over the period to which they are applicable. [Sec 706(d)(2)(A)]

   d. **Potential abuse:** Where a partner enters a partnership during the year, that partner may be allocated all losses or expenses, or a portion thereof, applicable to the entire period for which that partner was a member of the partnership. [*Mary K. Ogden*, 84 TC 871 (1985)]

      1) **Example:** The XY partnership admits partner Z on July 1. During the first six months of the year the partnership losses were $4,000. During the second six months the partnership losses were $8,000. The entire $8,000 loss may properly be allocated to Z.

VI.

PARTNERSHIP LOSSES

A. PARTNERSHIP INTEREST BASIS

1. **Limitation:** A partner's distributive share of partnership losses is allowed to the extent of his adjusted partnership interest basis. [Sec 704(d)]

   a. **Timing:** The determination of available basis is made at the end of the partnership year in which such loss occurred. All positive adjustments {Sec 705(a)(1)} are made first, followed by all negative adjustments {Sec 705(a)(2)} with the exception of share of losses. [Reg 1.704-1(d)(1)]

   b. **Excess:** Any excess loss is allowed at the end of the first partnership taxable year in which the partner has a positive basis after the above adjustments. [Reg 1.704-1(d)(1)]

2. **Effect of Liabilities:** Partnership interest basis is increased (decreased) by an increase (decrease) in respective share of partnership liabilities. [Sec 752(a)&(b)]

3. **Loss Denied:** Where a partner restored a negative capital account balance to a partnership subsequent to terminating his partnership interest, previously suspended losses were not deductible since he was not a partner at the time of payment. [*William Sennett*, 80 TC 825 (1983), aff'd per curriam, 752 F2d 428 (9th Cir 1985)]

4. See Part III for detailed discussion of partnership interest basis.

B. "AT RISK"

1. **Definition**

    a. Inclusions: Amounts considered at risk include money, basis of property contributed, and borrowed amounts on which the partner has pledged property or has personal liability. [Sec 465(b)(1)&(2)]

        1) Capital contributions: An amount that a partner is required to contribute to the partnership will not be considered at risk until actually paid. [Reg 1.465-22(a)]

        2) Qualified nonrecourse financing: Nonrecourse debt qualifies as "at risk" if it meets the following conditions:

            a) incurred on real property,

            b) borrowed from a qualified lender,

            c) not acquired from a related person,

            d) no person is personally liable, and

            e) the debt is not convertible. [Sec 465(b)(6)(B)]

    b. Exclusions: Amounts not considered at risk include loans from persons, other than creditors, with an interest in the same activity, or amounts on which the taxpayer is protected from loss. [Sec 465(b)(3)&(4)]

2. Limitation: An individual may deduct losses from an activity only to the extent she is at risk with respect to such activity. [Sec 465(a)(1)]

    a. Timing: A taxpayer's at risk amount is determined at the close of the taxable year of the partnership. [Sec 465(a)(1)]

    b. Excess: Any losses not allowed are suspended and carried over to subsequent years when the taxpayer is again at risk. [Sec 465(a)(2)]

        1) Gain on sale: A subsequent gain on the sale of the partnership interest may be offset by previously suspended losses. [Reg 1.465-66]

        2) Transfer of suspended losses

            a) Gift: A donor's share of unused suspended losses is added to the donee's basis, but does not increase the donee's at risk amount. [Reg 1.465-67]

            b) Sale: There is no provision in the Code or Regulations dealing with the transfer of suspended losses to a purchaser. Since the donor never suffered economic detriment with regard to the suspended loss, any transfer should be disallowed.

C. PASSIVE LOSSES

1. Rule: Losses from passive trade or business activities may only be deducted against passive income from such activities. [Sec 469(a)(1)(A)]

2. Application: Rules regarding passive losses are applied at the partner level, rather than the partnership level, and are beyond the scope of this outline.

20. What adverse consequences can occur as a result of continuation after termination?
21. What happens when two or more partnerships merge or consolidate?
22. How about when one partnership splits into two or more partnerships?
23. Bunching of partnership income:
    (a) What is the problem and how does it arise?
    (b) Is there any way to avoid this problem?
24. Will the entry of a new partner (through capital contributions) who receives more than 50% of profits and capital terminate the partnership year?

IX. PARTNERSHIP–PARTNER TRANSACTIONS

1. What is the general rule of section 707(a)?
2. What typical transactions will this include?
3. When are section 707(a) payments included in a partner's income?
4. What are guaranteed payments?
5. What treatment is accorded these payments?
6. When are these payments included in a partner's income?
7. Sections 707(a) and (c) both deal with payments to partners. What is the important difference between them?
8. With regard to personal services, when will the payments fall under section 707(a); section 707(c)?
9. With regard to interest paid, when will the payments fall under section 707(a); section 707(c)?
10. Is the partner considered an employee when he receives a guaranteed salary?
11. What is the difference between a guaranteed payment and a guaranteed minimum?
12. What is the restriction on losses in section 707(b)(1)?
13. Is the loss disallowed gone forever?
14. Who is entitled to the offset?
15. The XYZ partnership, in which X owns a 70% interest, sells property at a loss of $1,000 to H, X's son. What is the result?
16. What is the restriction on capital gains in section 707(b)(2)?
17. What important impact does section 267 have on payments between the partnership and its partners?

X. TRANSFERS OF PARTNERSHIP INTERESTS

1. What is the character of gain or loss recognized on the sale of a partnership interest?
2. What is the section 751 exception?
3. What constitutes the amount realized on a sale of a partnership interest?
4. What basis adjustments must the seller make?
5. What is the basis of the interest in the hands of the purchaser?

6. What effect does the sale/purchase have on the basis of partnership assets?
7. How is liquidation of a partner's interest treated under the code?
8. What is the determining factor in how the transaction of withdrawal is structured, i.e., sale or liquidation?
9. How is intent determined in ambiguous situations?
10. Does the Service care whether the transaction is structured as a sale or liquidation of a partner's interest?
11. A complete sale of the partnership could be treated as a sale of partnership assets or a sale of partnership interests. What tax consequences are involved?
12. How does the "Going Out of Business" doctrine affect partnerships, i.e. when does a sale constitute a sale of assets and when does it constitute a sale of partnership interests?
13. What does section 1031(a) provide and how does it affect partnership interests?
14. Does Rev. Rul. 84-115 override section 1031 so that an exchange of one partnership interest for another in a different partnership results in no gain or loss recognition?
15. Is abandonment considered a sale or exchange?
16. Can a gift be considered a sale or exchange?

XI. PARTNERSHIP HOT ASSETS

1. What is the general definition of unrealized receivables?
2. Does that mean accrual basis taxpayers will not encounter a problem here?
3. Do the above have any tax basis?
4. What constitutes "inventory"?
5. When are inventory items considered substantially appreciated?
6. Why is money excluded in the 10% test?
7. Are there any other methods you can think of to beat the 10% test?
8. Is the "substantially appreciated" test determined item-by-item or in the aggregate?
9. How is the gain or loss on section 751 property determined?
10. How is the selling price of each item of property determined?
11. How is basis in section 751 assets determined?
12. A and B are equal partners in the AB partnership. AB's balance sheet is as follows:

Assets	FMV	Basis
Cash	$10,000	$10,000
Accounts Receivable	20,000	0
Inventory	30,000	15,000
Machine ($10,000 in Depr.)	30,000	20,000
Total	$90,000	$45,000
Liabilities & Capital		
Notes Payable	25,000	25,000
Capital—A	32,500	10,000
Capital—B	32,500	10,000
Total	$90,000	$45,000

A sells his interest to C for $29,500 cash.

(a) What amount has A received for his partnership interest?
(b) What is A's basis in his partnership interest?
(c) What is total fair market value of section 751 property?
(d) Apply the test for substantially appreciated inventory. What are the figures?
(e) How much has A received for section 751 property?
(f) What is A's basis in section 751 property?
(g) What is the amount and character of A's gain?

XII. PARTNERSHIP DISTRIBUTIONS

1. Distinguish "current" from "liquidating" distributions.
2. What effect does a distribution have on recognition of gain or loss by the partnership?
3. When does a partner recognize a gain on distribution?
4. When does a partner recognize loss on a distribution?
5. How is the loss determined?
6. What is the character of gain or loss recognized under section 731(a)?
7. Since income is considered earned on the last day of the partnership year, will withdrawals in excess of basis cause recognition of a gain? Explain.
8. What is the basis of property received in a "current" distribution?
9. Partner A has a $10,000 basis in his partnership interest. He receives a "current" distribution of property (FMV of $8,000 and basis of $6,000 to the partnership) plus $3,000 in cash.
   (a) What gain or loss is recognized?
   (b) What is his basis in the property?
   (c) What is his basis in his partnership interest?
10. In (9) above what if the basis to the partnership of the property had been $8,000?
11. What is the basis of property distributed in a "liquidating" distribution? Any limitations?
12. How is basis allocated when sections 732(a)(2) or 732(b) are applicable?
13. Partner A has a $17,000 basis in his partnership interest. He receives the following liquidating distribution:
    Cash—$2,000
    Inventory—FMV of $3,500, basis of $3,000
    Capital asset—FMV of $3,000, basis of $2,000
    Depreciable asset—FMV of $6,000, basis of $4,000
    What is A's basis in the property?
14. On subsequent disposition is all recognized gain or loss capital in nature if sections 751 and 736 do not apply to a distribution?
15. If a partner receives inventory items and holds them more than 5 years does he then recognize capital treatment?
16. Can the distributee partner tack the partnership holding period of the inventory to his holding period?
17. How are withdrawals against future income treated?

XIII. DISPROPORTIONATE DISTRIBUTIONS

1. When does section 751(b) apply?
2. What is the fiction created by regulation 1.751-1(b)?
3. Are there any distributions to which section 751(b) is not applicable?
4. What determines the character of gain recognized by the partner or partnership in a disproportionate distribution?
5. If a partner receives a disproportionate distribution as a current distribution is he allocated any gain recognized by the partnership?
6. The XYZ partnership has assets consisting only of cash and substantially appreciated inventory. It distributes cash to X in liquidation of his interest. Has X sold his share of inventory to the partnership?

   (a) How would this distribution affect partnership basis in inventory?

   (b) How is excess cash received by X determined?

   (c) If the partnership had distributed inventory instead of cash would there still be a sale?

7. Assume that a partnership has the following assets:

	Basis	FMV
Cash	$6,000	$6,000
Inventory	6,000	9,000
Land	9,000	12,000

   C, an equal 1/3 partner, receives $2,000 cash and inventory worth $7,000 in liquidation of his partnership interest. (The partnership has no liabilities.)

   (a) What is the amount of inventory considered sold by the partnership?

   (b) What is the sales price of the land?

   (c) What is C's basis in the land sold?

   (d) What is the basis to the partnership of the inventory considered sold?

   (e) What amount of gain is recognized by C and by the partnership?

8. What treatment is accorded "hot assets" distributed in transactions not falling under section 751(b)?

9.

	Adj. Basis	FMV
ASSETS		
Cash	$15,000	$15,000
Accounts Receivable	15,000	15,000
Inventory	30,000	45,000
Land	30,000	45,000
	$90,000	$120,000
LIAB. & CAPITAL		
Current Liabilities	15,000	15,000
Mortgage Pay	30,000	30,000
Capital		
A	15,000	25,000
B	15,000	25,000
C	15,000	25,000
	$90,000	$120,000

"A" received land worth $15,000 plus $10,000 in cash in liquidation. What are the tax consequences?

10. Schedule out the answer (as above) for:
    (a) Example 2 in regulation 1.751-1(g).
    (b) Example 3 in regulation 1.751-1(g).

XIV. PAYMENTS TO RETIRED AND DECEASED PARTNERS

1. Section 736 splits payments into two categories. Describe these categories generally.

2. How is the determination made of which category a payment falls into?

3. How is value determined with regard to liquidations?

4. Which category does a payment for unrealized receivables fall into?

5. What type of gain is recognized on a section 736(b) payment?

6. What category do goodwill payments fall into?

7. What about previously purchased goodwill? Which category?

8. If payments are made in installments, what portion of the payments are considered property payments:
    (a) When payments are fixed?
    (b) When payments are not fixed in amount?
    (c) When total payments are fixed and more than the agreed annual amount is paid in any year?
    (d) When less than the apportioned amount of a section 736(b) payment is received in any year?

9. For reporting purposes must fixed payments under section 736(b) be prorated between basis recovery and gain?

10. If a taxpayer must report income from section 736(b) payments, in what year does he include such income?

11. What does section 736(a) provide?

12. Is it really necessary to distinguish "distributive share" and "guaranteed payments" in section 736(a); aren't they both ordinary income payments?

13. How do you determine which category the section 736(a) payments fall into?

14. In what year does a recipient of section 736(a) payments report the income?

15. Is the partnership entitled to a deduction for section 736(a) payments; section 736(b) payments?

XV. SPECIAL BASIS ADJUSTMENTS

1. If property with a partnership tax basis of $6,000 is distributed to a partner who has a $4,000 basis in his partnership interest, what is the partner's basis in the distributed property?

2. Is the $2,000 difference lost to the partner?

3. If prior to the distribution the tax bases of assets equaled the partners' bases in their partnership interests, would they still be equal after the distribution?

4. If the partnership above then sells all the property in which the withdrawing partner relinquished an interest, would the result be equitable? Why?

5. Is there any way for the partnership to recover the lost $2,000 in basis?

6. Section 754 provides for an election to adjust basis. Where do you look to determine what specific adjustments are to be made?

7. Can a partnership make a section 754 election for a section 734(b) adjustment only?

8. Must the election be made each year?

9. When must the section 754 election be made?

10. What determines the basis of a purchased partnership interest?

11. What will usually determine the cost of the partnership interest?

12. Will the purchasing partner have a basis for his partnership interest different from his share of partnership basis in the assets?

13. If the purchaser paid $10,000 for a 1/4 interest in a partnership owning only land with a basis of $30,000, what would be the purchaser's share of the basis in the land?

14. If the partnership sold the land for $40,000, how much profit would the purchasing partner report?

15. If the purchaser had purchased 1/4 of the partnership land above at its fair market value of $10,000 and then sold it at that fair market value, he would have had no gain. Is it fair that he should pay tax on the gain when he has not in fact realized any gain? Will he ever be able to offset this artificial gain?

16. What is the purpose of a section 754 election?

17. How is the basis adjustment in a transfer determined?

18. How is the transferee partner's proportionate share of partnership asset basis determined?

19. Who is entitled to the basis adjustment in a transfer?

20. What happens when property subject to a special basis adjustment is distributed to a partner who is not entitled to the basis adjustment?

21. How is a basis adjustment increase in a distribution determined?

22. How is a decrease in basis adjustment in a distribution determined?

23. Who is entitled to the basis adjustment under section 734(b)?

24. What happens when a partner receives a distribution of property on which he is unable to utilize his entire special basis adjustment that previously was obtained under section 743(b)?

25. What is the first step in allocating a special basis adjustment determined under section 734(b) or section 743(b)?

26. How is the amount to be allocated to each class determined:
    (a) in a transfer?
    (b) in a distribution?

27. In an allocation within a class, how is the allocation to be made?

28. If the partnership fails to make a section 754 election, is a transferee partner:
    (a) Entitled to make the election?
    (b) When must the election be made?

(c) How is the adjustment made?

29. If a transferee partner is unable to use his special basis adjustment under section 732(d), can the partnership utilize such?

ANSWERS

I. WHAT CONSTITUTES A PARTNERSHIP

1. The Code definition is quite similar and can be broken out into two elements:
   (a) Some combination of taxpayers for conducting business,
   (b) Which is not a corporation, trust, or estate.
   The big difference between the two definitions is profit motive. The U.P.A. specifically requires a profit motive, while the Code and Reg are silent about it.

2. McKee seems to think that a profit motive is required {paragraph 3.02[3]}. In Ian T. Allison, 35 TCM 1069 (1976), lack of a profit motive was fatal. However, the court in *Madison Gas* specifically states that "the statute does not require a profit motive."

3. Federal tax law usually supersedes state law; however, state law usually is considered in defining what falls within the federal law. Although there appears to be a major conflict between state and federal law here, there really is not. Since the federal definition is broader, it easily encompasses the rule laid out in the Uniform Partnership Act. Therefore, state law should merely be a factor in determining whether or not a particular organization constitutes a partnership. [Reg 301.7701-1(b)]

4. Intent—arrived at by considering all the relevant factors. This main test overruled the *Tower* case in which a prior list of objective standards had been established.

5. Not at all. It is the intent to carry on a joint business enterprise.

6. No, they are only factors to be considered. The rule of *Culbertson* still controls today.

7. Section 761(b) defines a partner as "a member of a partnership." The more important question concerns who can be a partner. Any person or entity may generally be a partner in a partnership.

8. Section 761(a) also provides for an organization to elect out of the Subchapter K provisions if the organization falls into one of the following three categories:

(1) investment purposes only,

(2) joint production, extraction, or use of property, or

(3) certain securities transactions by dealers.

Regulation 1.761-2 sets forth the specifics with regard to this election.

9. Reg 301.7701-2 lists six factors to be used in determining what constitutes an association. Since the first two factors are common to both partnerships and corporations, they are excluded in the test and only the last four are considered. If the organization possesses more than two of these four characteristics, it will be an association taxed as a corporation. [Reg 301.7701-2(a)(3)]

10. When death, insanity, bankruptcy, retirement, resignation, or expulsion of any member will not cause a dissolution of the organization. [Reg 301.7701-2(b)(1)]

11. A dissolution is a change of identity of an organization as a result of a change in the relationship between its members.[Reg 301.7701-2(b)(2)] A termination is the ending of the business, rather than a mere change in relationship among the owners.

12. Yes, this factor will not be found to be present if the partnership is in compliance with either the Uniform Partnership Act or the Uniform Limited Partnership Act. [Reg 301.77012(b)(3)]

13. Exclusive authority to make management decisions necessary to conduct the business, held by any one person or group of persons of less than all the members. [Reg 301.7701-2(c)(1)]

14. Once again compliance with either the U.P.A. or U.L.P.A. will guarantee avoidance of this factor. However, the limited partners must not own substantially all the interests in the partnership, i.e., ownership or control of all the general partnership interests. [Reg 301.7701-2(c)(4)]

15. Where no member of the partnership is personally liable for partnership debts under local law. [Reg 301.7701-2(d)(1)]

16. Yes, unless no general partner has any substantial assets which could be reached by creditors *AND* is merely acting as a "dummy" agent of the limited partners. [Reg 301.7701-2(d)(1)&(2)]

17. Yes, according to a literal reading of the Regs (note the conjunctive). *Larson v Commissioner,* 66 TC 159 (1976), reaches the same conclusion.

18. A general partner who is under the control of the limited partners (*Larson*); one who has no substantial assets (*Glensder Textile*); and agent of the limited partners (*Zuckman*).

The *Glensder* definition is clearly wrong, as it ignores the conjunctive requirement. It is easy to argue that there is little difference between the *Larson* and *Zuckman* definitions in substance. State agency law imputes legal liability from the agent to the principal and the Uniform Partnership Act imputes legal liability to a limited partner who exercises management control. If the limited partners control the general partner, then they may be held liable for the debts of the partnership under either or both of the above theories. Since the limited partners would be liable for the debts of the partnership, there would be unlimited liability and therefore, the factor of limited liability could not be present any time the limited partners controlled the general partner.

19. Not if the transfer results in a dissolution. [Reg 301.77012(e)(1)]

20. Yes, but only as elements of the other major factors discussed above. [Rev Rul 79-106, 1979-1 CB 448 and *Larson*]

II. PARTNERSHIP FORMATION

1. No. Section 721 applies any time a partner makes a property contribution in exchange for a partnership interest when he is acting in the capacity of a partner. [Reg 1.721-1(a)]

2. No. A partner may receive boot without recognizing gain, if such does not constitute proceeds from a sale of the property. [Reg 1.721-1(a)]

3. It is equal to the sum of (1) adjusted basis of contributed assets, (2) money contributed, and (3) any gain recognized under section 721(b). [Sec 722]

4. The partnership takes the same basis the contributing partner had in the asset immediately before the contribution, increased by the amount of any gain the partner recognizes on the transaction under section 721(b). [Sec 723]

5. Any increase in a partner's share of liabilities is treated as a contribution of money by the partner [Sec 752(a)]. Any decrease in a partner's share of liabilities is treated as a money distribution to the partner [Sec 752(b)]. The change in liabilities, of course, will change the basis of the partnership interest as well.

6. Section 752(b) provides that any decrease in a partner's share of liabilities will be treated as money distributed and section 731(a)(1) states that any money received in excess of basis will result in gain to the extent thereof. Therefore, if the portion of liabilities the contributing partner is released from exceeds the basis of all property contributed by that partner, he must recognize gain to the extent of the excess.

7. Partnership: The partnership may always tack the partner's holding period on contributed property. [See Reg 1.1223-1(b)]

   Partner: A partner may tack the period for which contributed assets were held only if they were either capital assets or section 1231(b) assets in the partner's hands at the time of contribution. [See Reg 1.1223-1(a)]

8. According to the regulation you can only tack when the basis is the same as it would have been in the hands of the other person. Since the partnership interest basis is determined with reference to the property contributed by the partner, regulation 1.1223-1(b) can't be applied to the partner's partnership interest.

9. There is no answer to this question. McKee raises the possibility of fragmented holding periods. The higher the percentage of non-capital assets contributed by a partner, the greater the chance the IRS will hold that there should be a fragmentation or possibly no tacking at all. For example, should a partner who contributes $100,000 in non-capital assets and $100 in capital assets be able to tack the holding period of his capital asset to his entire partnership interest?

10. To the extent gain is recognized recapture must be recognized to the extent thereof. If no gain is recognized the recapture attributes attach to the assets and carry over to the partnership.

11. Section 38 property does not cease to be such by mere change in the form of a business operation as long as the taxpayer retains a substantial interest in the business. The contributing partner will be subject to recapture upon early disposition of section 38 property. [Sec 47(b)]

12. (a) Probably not; in the corporate area the Third Circuit held that assignment-of-income would not prevail over nonrecognition of gain under section 351 [*Hempt Bros. v. United States*, 490 F2d 1172(1974)]. The Service has acquiesced to *Hempt* in Rev

Rul 80-198, 1980-2 CB 122. It is logical to assume the same result under Subchapter K.

(b) Again, we can look to the corporate area for guidance here, as there is no answer in a partnership context. While amended section 357(c) applies only to corporations, the holding in the case of *Donald D. Focht,* 68 TC 22 (1977), should serve as good precedent. In *Focht,* the court held that where accounts receivable (with zero basis) exceeded accounts payable, the accounts payable would not be treated as liabilities for purposes of section 357(c). The Conference Committee stated in H Rep No 98-861, 98th Cong, 2d Sess (1984), that accrued payables are not to be treated as liabilities for purposes of section 752 .

(c) Don't transfer accounts payable. Alternatively, have the transferring partner retain equal amounts of accounts receivable and accounts payable. The net worth of the sole proprietorship will remain the same and therefore not upset the value of his contribution.

13. No. The determination of whether a sale or exchange has occurred must still be made according to the guidelines set out in *Otey.*

14. No, exchanges of services are not considered property, but rather are considered taxable exchanges. [See sections 83(a) and 707(a)(2)]

15. It appears to exclude capital interests received for services (but not profits interests) from the general non-recognition provisions of Sec 721; i.e., it says an exchange of services for capital is taxable.

16. When the other partners give up any right to be repaid a part of their capital contributions. [Reg 1.721-1(b)(1)]

17. Where property is transferred in exchange for services, the person contributing services recognizes ordinary income to the extent the fair market value of the property received exceeds the amount paid. Such is taxable in the first year in which the interest is transferable, or not subject to a substantial risk of forfeiture.

18. Both Willis and McKee seem to think so, but there is a potential argument that a "profits" interest may not be property under the definition at Reg 1.83-3(e). (Note that section 83(a) is phrased as "property for services.")

19. If section 83(a) does not apply, the taxpayer may elect to be taxed on the excess of fair market value of the property (capital interest) received over the amount paid.

20. Where there is subsequent capital appreciation, the taxpayer will generally be taxed at capital gain rates on the appreciation, rather than having such taxed as ordinary income from services.

21. (a) How fair market value is to be determined.

(b) Subsequent forfeiture prior to vesting yields no deduction for any prior basis increase resulting from ordinary income recognition under section 83(b). [Reg 1.83-2(a)]

22. Whoever the service was rendered to; i.e., either the other partner(s) or the partnership [Reg 1.721-1(b)(2) and Reg 1.83-6(a)(1)]. Normally this can be answered by asking when the services were performed.

23. Yes, capitalization of the amount paid is required under section 263 where the services constitute a capital asset (e.g., construction services with regard to property development). [Sec 707(c)]

24. Absent an allocation under section 704, each partner will receive his proportionate share. This will usually result in a detriment to the other partners, since the contributing partner should not be entitled to any portion of the deduction.

25. Reg 1.83-1(a)(1)(ii) provides that property received subject to restrictions belongs to the transferor (partner giving up capital interest) until vested in the transferee. However, any income received by the transferee will be treated as compensation for services in the year received or made available.

26. Reg 1.83-6(b), added by the 1976 Reform Act, makes it clear that the Service takes the position that the appreciation on the transferred portion will be taxed to the transferor. Note that *McDougal v Commissioner,* 45 TC 588 (1974), which was decided prior to the 1976 Reform Act, reached a similar result. The transfer was deemed to have been made to the other partner prior to the contribution to the partnership by both parties; therefore, the transferor partner, rather than the partnership, recognized the gain.

III. PARTNERSHIP INTEREST BASIS

1. Section 705(a) provides that it is section 722 or section 742 basis:

Plus partner's share of:	Minus:
a. Taxable income	a. Distributions to partner
b. Tax exempt income	b. Partner's share of losses
c. Excess depletion (over basis of property depleted)	c. Partner's share of non-deductible expenses
	d. Partner's share of depletion deduction (limited to basis)

2. It doesn't need to since section 752(a) and (b) combined with sections 705(a) and 722 will cause such to be included. Section 752(a) provides that an increase in liabilities will be treated as a cash contribution, thus increasing basis under section 722. Section 752(b) provides that a decrease in liabilities will be treated as a cash distribution, thus decreasing basis under section 705(a).

3. Section 742 provides that basis of a partnership interest acquired other than by contribution is determined under Subchapter O (normal basis rules). Note that the starting point for section 705 is section 742 (and/or section 722).

4. No, section 705(a) provides that the reductions to basis may never reduce basis below zero.

5. (a) Yes, section 705(b) provides that a partner may determine his basis by reference to his proportionate share of partnership asset basis as prescribed by Reg 1.705-1(b)

   (b) Not necessarily. Contributions of appreciated property, sales or exchanges of partnership interests, and special allocations constitute some of the factors which can complicate the adjustment.

   (c) When the general rule of section 705(a) cannot practically be applied or when in the Commissioner's opinion the result obtained will not vary substantially from the general rule. [Reg 1.705- 1(b)]

   (d) Only in the simplest of situations. (Note that this will be equal to proportionate share of asset basis because of the basic accounting equation.) Many of the same (if not all) factors discussed in (c) above will require certain adjustments to be made to this basic formula.

6. According to her loss-sharing ratio. [Reg 1.752-1(e)]

7. (a) A limited partner's share of recourse liability cannot exceed any additional contributions he is obligated to make under the partnership agreement. [Reg 1.752-1(e)]
   (b) If debt is nonrecourse then all partners will share "according to their profit ratio". [1.752-1(e)]

8. See the example in Reg 1.752-1(e).

9. McKee reasons that nonrecourse debt will only be repaid if the partnership is profitable. Therefore the partners should share according to their profit ratios.

10. Yes, according to Rev Rul 60-345. However, the Conference Committee stated otherwise in H Rep No 861.

11. No, since no liability has been fixed. For example see *Albany Car Wheel Co.*, 40 TC 831 (1963).

12. Secondary liability is best considered a contingent liability that has not been fixed. In the hypothetical case, the primary debtor and the property securing the debt should both precede AB's liability, thus making remote the possibility of AB having to pay.

13. These terms relate to partnership agreements that include a provision for a change in profit and loss ratios at some point in time.

14. Often it is used in limited partnerships. It allows the limited partners to deduct early losses, then recover contributions, and maybe share in subsequent income or appreciation.

15. At the point of the "flip" in profit and loss sharing ratios, section 752(b) in conjunction with section 731(a) may cause certain partners to recognize income strictly from the change in ratios.

IV. PARTNERSHIP TAX LIABILITY

1. The partners, in their individual capacities as a partnership, are not subject to income tax. [Sec 701]

2. Gross income, deductions, distributive shares (of income, gain, loss, deduction, or credit), and names and addresses of all partners. [Reg 1.6031-1(a)(1)]

3. Any one of the partners. His signature is evidence of his authority to sign. [Sec 6063]

4. $50.00 per partner per month for a maximum of five months. [Sec 6698]

5. (a) Items that must be stated separately under Sec 702(a); [Sec 703(a)(1)] AND
   (b) Certain deductions not allowed to a partnership. [Sec 703(a)(2)]

6. (a) Any items that are specially allocated under the partnership agreement. [Reg 1.702-1(a)(8)(i)]
   (b) Any item which will cause a different tax liability to any partner if not separately stated. [Reg 1.702- 1(a)(8)(ii)] Even though the item may affect only one partner's tax liability, the item must be stated separately for all partners.

Note: Section 702(a)(7) is catchall and section 702(a)(8) refers to partnership taxable income.

7. To preserve the character of these items and thereby prevent distortions or abuses that would result from consolidations.

8. Yes, section 702(c) says "distributive", not "distributed". Reg 1.702-1(a) says "whether or not distributed."

9. According to most cases, but some have taken the position that the income was not income to the partnership, but rather income solely to the partner perpetrating the fraud (an argument worthy of consideration).

10. It depends on whether the partnership interest constitutes separate property or community property. If community property, each is required to report one-half. [Reg 1.702-1(d)]

11. The language of section 702(b) is not clear in this respect. Two cases, *Podell*, 55 TC 429, and *Stivers*, 32 TCM 1139, and Reg 1.702-1(b) indicate character is determined at the partnership level and passes through to the individual partners. See also Rev Rul 68-79, 1968-1 CB 310.

12. It would appear so, as Reg 1.702-1(b) says "any" item described in section 702(a)(1) through (8), thereby including all items of income, deductions, and credits.

13. At the partner level. Since the character passes through, the partner will then make a determination of the tax status of each item as it relates to such partner. Rev Rul 75-523, 1975-2 CB 257, serves as an excellent example, but may raise the argument that character is determined at the partner level!

14. To prevent double deductions and also to prevent distortion of income at the individual partner's level.

15. Section 703(b) specifies that all elections shall be made at the partnership level except for the three listed therein. There are other exceptions (See McKee, section 9.04).

16. Method of accounting, taxable year, and installment sale reporting to mention just a few.

17. Certain desired tax benefits may be lost if the partnership is not able to change its election or deemed election; e.g., partners who desire tax-free "like-kind" exchanges under section 1031 cannot elect such treatment on partnership exchanges where the partnership itself failed to make the election.

18. Section 706(b) provides that a partnership may not adopt or change to a taxable year different from the majority of its partners without a business purpose and permission by the Commissioner. Likewise, a partner may not change his taxable year to one other than that of the partnership.

19. The partnership must adopt a calendar year. [Sec 706 (b)]

V. PARTNERSHIP ALLOCATIONS

1. As determined by the partnership agreement under section 704(a), the partners may allocate any item in any manner they choose.

2. Yes, section 761(c) states that the partnership agreement includes any modifications made up to the time for filing the return, excluding extensions.

3. Section 704(b). A partner's share is determined in accordance with his interest in the partnership.

4. The old regulations [Reg 1.704-1(b)(1)] said to look to the actual amounts credited on the partnership books. Although this language has been deleted from the new regula-

tions, amounts credited to the capital accounts of the partners on the partnership books should be evidence of an agreement.

5. Each will report $4,000 ordinary loss and $4,500 capital gain. Since there is no agreement with regard to capital gains and losses, such will be shared according to the general profit ratio even though the items are separately stated. Note that the manner in which the partners actually split is the critical factor here. Obviously the partners were not concerned about character, but rather only the economics as evidenced by their equal split.

6. By specifying in the agreement that (1) all allocations will be reflected in the partners' capital accounts, (2) liquidating distributions will be according to positive capital account balances, and (3) all partners are unconditionally required to restore any deficit balance in their capital account upon liquidation. [Reg 1.704-1(b)(2)(ii)(b)]

7. No. The allocation causes a shift in tax consequences that substantially outweighs the shift in economic consequences. A has a net increase after tax of $8000, compared to $7500 if both items are split equally. B is in the same position, both economically and tax-wise under both allocations.

8. No. The allocations are merely transitory since the income allocations offset the deduction within five years. [Reg 1.704-1(b)(2)(iii)(c)]

9. No. Revaluation upon entry of a new partner is elective, not mandatory. [Reg 1.704-1(b)(2)(iv)]

10. Depreciation, depletion, gain, or loss on contributed property shall be allocated in a manner so as to take into account the variation between basis and fair market value.

11. (a) The partnership recognizes $100 income and each partner recognizes his $50 share. A has been taxed on $50 of B's precontribution income. [See Reg. 1.704-1(c)(1)]

    (b)

	A	B
Pre-sale basis	$1,000	$ 900
Gain recognized	50	50
Post-sale basis	1,050	950
Liquidation proceeds	1,000	1,000
Gain (Loss) on liquidation	(50)	50

    A now gets to recognize a $50 loss, but such will be a capital loss. A broke even economically, but traded $50 of ordinary gain for $50 of capital loss. B will recognize a $50 capital gain. He also broke even economically (assuming he could have sold the inventory himself for $1,000), but exchanged $50 in ordinary gain for $50 in capital gain. Note the timing inequity also, as A is not made economically whole until his interest is sold or otherwise liquidated.

    (c) Allocate all $100 precontribution income to B.

	A	B
Pre-sale basis	$1,000	$ 900
Gain recognized on		
Sale of inventory	0	100
Post-sale basis	1,000	1,000
Liquidation proceeds	1,000	1,000
Gain (Loss) on liquidation	0	0

12. No. Retroactive allocations of pre-entry items are not allowed. Allocations must be made according to the partners' varying interests during the taxable year.

13. No. The Tax Reform Act of 1984 provides that cash basis partnerships must use accrual methods for determining the allocation of revenues and expenses. The allocation must consider the length of time that the partner was a member of the partnership.

VI. PARTNERSHIP LOSSES

1. Section 704(d) provides that losses will be allowed only to the extent of a partner's adjusted basis in his partnership interest.
2. At the end of the partnership year in which it is incurred. [Sec 704(d)]
3. It is allowed as a deduction at the end of any partnership year in which the partner increases his basis above zero. [Sec 704(d)]
4. Yes. Section 752(a) treats an increase in liabilities as a contribution of money which results in a basis increase.
5. Section 465(a)(1) provides that individuals may deduct losses from an activity only to the extent they are "at risk" with respect to such activity at the close of the taxable year.
6. (a) Money. [Sec 465(b)(1)(B)]
   (b) Adjusted basis of contributed property. [Sec 465(b)(1)(B)]
   (c) Borrowed amounts on which there is
      1) personal liability [Sec 465(b)(2)(A)] or
      2) pledged property other than property used in the activity. [Sec 465(b)(2)(B)]
7. (a) Certain borrowed amounts from a person who
      1) has an interest in such activity or
      2) has a section 168(e)(4) relationship. [Sec 465(b)(3)]
   (b) Amounts protected through
      1) nonrecourse financing,
      2) guarantees,
      3) stop loss agreements, or
      4) other similar arrangments. [Sec 465(b)(4)]
8. Section 465(b)(6) specifically excludes the holding of real property from the "at risk" provisions if such is financed with qualified nonrecourse debt.
9. Section 465(a)(2) provides for a carryover of such losses to subsequent years when basis is restored. Note this parallels the treatment accorded under section 704(d).
10. Yes, in a roundabout fashion. Section 704(a) permits allocation in any manner that has substantial economic effect. The problem with such allocations is that the partner being allocated the additional loss will also suffer additional economic burden unless subsequent gains are charged back to the same partner.
11. Yes. Reg 1.465-66 provides that any gain recognized on a transfer will be treated as income against which any previously suspended losses may be deducted.
12. There is no specific language dealing with this problem in the regulations. The reasonable answer should be no, as the taxpayer never suffered any economic detriment by reason of the suspended loss. Any basis for nonrecourse debt remaining should be offset by release of such liabilities upon transfer.
13. Reg 1.465-67 provides that such suspended losses will be added to the transferor's basis. Since the transferee's basis is determined with reference to the transferor's basis, the

transferee thereby obtains a step-up in basis for the suspended losses. The transferee should not be able to offset this basis with losses however, since she would not be at risk with regard to such basis.

14. (a) Have partners make year-end contributions (to increase basis),
    (b) Don't make year-end contributions (to carry loss over), or
    (c) Make withdrawals (to lower basis for purposes of loss carryover).

15. Yes. Reg 1.465-4 sets out the general guidelines. They might attack under either the "step transaction" or "business purpose" doctrines.

16. A tiered partnership exists where one partnership owns a partnership interest in another partnership. There is no limit on the number of tiers in the complete structure. Rev Rul 77-309 provides that any partner (including a partnership) will be allocated his share of nonrecourse debt for purposes of determining basis under section 704(d). The at-risk rules will apply at the individual level.

17. Section 705(a) determines adjusted basis, section 704(d) limits losses to the adjusted basis determined under section 705(a), and section 465 limits the amount of losses that may be deducted for tax purposes.

VII. FAMILY PARTNERSHIPS

1. Income may not be assigned to another for tax purposes. Income from services is taxed to the person who provides the services (*Lucas v Earl*) and income from capital is taxed to the owner of the capital (*Horst*). However, income from capital can be shifted by also transferring the capital which produces the income. [*Blair v Commissioner*, 300 US 5 (1937)]

2. A person shall be recognized as a partner if he owns a capital interest which is a material income producing factor. Note also that the ownership may be acquired by either purchase or gift. The language should not be read to exclude other acquisitions, e.g., inheritance.

3. No. It still applies where capital is not a material income producer or where a partner does not own any capital (See *Carriage Square*).

4. The transferee must have dominion and control over the transferred interest. [Reg 1.704-1(e)(1)(iii)]

5. Substantial participation in management and control of the business [Reg 1.704-1(e)(2)(iv)] and the distribution to the donee partner of his share of income for his sole benefit and use. [Reg 1.704-1(e)(2)(v)]

6. Interests acquired from family members by purchase [Sec 704(e)(2)] or gift may not be allocated income generated by the donor's services or income disproportionate to his capital interest.

7. It appears that the Service is taking that position in Reg 1.704-1(e)(3)(i)(b), since it states that income shall be allocated "between the donor and donee in accordance with their respective interests in partnership capital." Note that this applies only to family members' shares.

8. Regulation 1.704-1(e)(1)(iv) says an interest is a material income producer if a substantial portion of gross income of the business is attributable to capital. Ordinarily, substantial investments in inventories and/or equipment will qualify.

VIII. PARTNERSHIP TERMINATIONS

1. Section 706(c)(1) provides that except in a termination, the partnership year will not close by reason of a partner's death, entry of a new partner, liquidation of a partner's entire interest, or sale or exchange of a partner's interest.

2. (a) A partnership year closes for a partner who sells, exchanges, or has his entire interest liquidated. [Sec 706(c)(2)]
   (b) A termination under section 708(b) (discussed below).

3. Regulation 1.706-1(c)(2)(ii) provides three different alternatives:
   (a) An interim closing of the books, if not otherwise agreed by the partners.
   (b) Pro-rata allocation.
   (c) Any other reasonable allocation.

4. The "pure" pro-rata approach is based on year-end amounts; however, any reasonable allocation is permissible. [Reg 1.7061(c)(2)(ii)] A variation of the pure pro-rata approach allocates operating items on a pro-rata approach and extraordinary items on the basis of when actually received (For an example see McKee, 11.02(5)(a)). An interim closing may be necessary for other purposes, i.e., to make adjustments under sections 734 or 743.

5. Regulation 1.706-1(c) (2)(ii) says "agreement among the partners" but does not specify whether the outgoing or incoming partners may participate. In order to avoid problems, Willis suggests that all partners participate in the agreement.

6. No, the above regulation specifies that he must use the same method as the transferor. This might suggest that he is not entitled to participate in the method chosen.

7. When a partner dies. [Sec 706-1(c)(2)(A)(ii)]

8. Regulation 1.706-1(c)(3)(ii) provides that the decedent will not include partnership income or loss up to the date of death for a partnership year which has not closed for the partnership.

9. Regulation 1.706-1(c)(3)(iv) provides that such results in a sale as of the date of death and that the year closes with respect to the deceased partner.

10. No. Regulation 1.706-1(c)(5) provides that the partnership year does not close with regard to either partner. However, the donor and donee partners must prorate their income (loss) in accordance with their capital interests governed by regulation 1.704-1(e)(3)(B).

11. According to his varying interests during the year, subject to the requirements set forth in section 706(d).

12. New section 706(d) and regulations to be published will govern. The basic premise is to assign income, loss etc., on a daily basis to partners whose interests changed during the year. Accrual methods must be used by cash basis partnerships in determining the amount of the allocation only.

13. Section 708(b) provides for a termination if no part of the business is continued by any of the partners as a partnership, or if within a 12-month period there is a sale or exchange of 50% or more of the total interests in profits and capital. Note that distributions are treated as exchanges under section 761(e).

14. Regulation 1.708-1(b)(1)(i) provides that such activity ceases when all assets are distributed. The courts are in agreement. See *Ginsburg,* 396 F2d 983 (Ct Cl 1968); *Foxman,* 41 TC 535 (1964); and *Baker Commodities,* 415 F2d 519 (9th Cir 1969).

15. Regulation 1.708-1(b) (1)(i)(a) says not if the estate or other successor continues to share in the profits and losses.

16. No. It must be 50% or more of the capital *AND* profits.

17. Yes, sale of more than 50% within 12 months. [Example from regulation 1.708-1(b)(1)(ii)]

18. No, since D simply resold A's interest. [Example in regulation above continued]

19. Regulation 1.708-1(b)(1)(iv) treats the transaction as if there had been a liquidating distribution with an immediate contribution by the continuing partners to a new partnership.

20. (a) Failure to make partnership elections.

   (b) Gain or loss may result from the hypothetical distribution.

   (c) Investment credit may have to be recaptured.

   (d) The tax year might be lost.

21. If the owners of one of the old partnerships own more than 50% of the capital and profits of the new partnership, it will be considered a continuation of such preceding partnership; otherwise, all previous partnerships have terminated and a new partnership is formed. [Reg 1.708-1(b)(2)(i)]

22. If the owners of one or more of the resulting partnerships previously owned more than 50% of the capital and profits of the previous partnership, then such new partnership(s) shall be considered a continuation of the old partnership. [Reg 1.7081(b)(2)(ii)]

23. (a) Where more than 12 months of partnership income is included in a partner's income for a particular year because the partnership year closes with respect to a partner who is on a different year-end. Example: Partner A on a calendar year in a partnership with a May 31 fiscal year sells his entire interest on Nov. 30. He must report his share of the income for the partnership's fiscal year plus his share for the period June 1 through Nov. 30, a total of 18 months' income.

   (b) 1) Sell the interest after the calendar year ends.

   2) Sell less than the entire interest prior to the partner's year end and the balance afterward.

24. No; Revenue Ruling 75-423 clarifies the Service's position on entry of a partner through capital contributions. The ruling emphasizes the language of regulation 1.708-1(b)(1)(ii), "contribution of property does not constitute a sale or exchange."

IX. PARTNERSHIP–PARTNER TRANSACTIONS

1. When a partner enters into a transaction with a partnership in which he is a member, the transaction will be treated as one taking place between the partnership and an outsider if the partner is not acting in the capacity of a partner.

2. Loans to or from the partnership, sales and purchases between the partners and the partnership, and services rendered to the partnership. [Reg 1.707-1(a)]

3. Since the partner is treated as not acting in a capacity as such, the recognition of income will depend upon his method of accounting, i.e., when received for a cash basis partner and when earned for an accrual basis partner.

4. Payments for services or the use of capital which are determined without regard to partnership income. [Sec 707(c)]

5. They are treated as ordinary income to the partner under section 61(a), and expenses to the partnership which are either expensed under section 162(a) or capitalized under section 263. [Sec 707(c)]

6. In the partner's taxable year with or within which ends the partnership taxable year for which the partnership is entitled to the deduction. [Reg 1.707-1(c)]
Note that this treatment is similar to the treatment for a partner's distributive share.

7. Timing of income recognition. Section 707(a) depends on the partner's accounting method, whereas section 707(c) depends on the partnership taxable year in which the payments are deductible according to the partnership's accounting method.

8. If the services are unrelated to performance of partnership business or are provided directly to the partnership they are section 707(a) payments. If the services result in revenue to the partnership they fall under section 707(c), since the partner is functioning in his capacity as a partner. Revenue Rulings 81-300 and 81-301 may be useful in making that distinction.

9. They will fall under section 707(a) when paid on a bona fide loan and under section 707(c) when paid on invested capital.

10. No. Guaranteed payments are considered such only for purposes of computing a partner's gross income and partnership expenses. For all other purposes they are considered as part of the partner's distributive share of ordinary income. [Reg 1.7071(c)]

11. A guaranteed payment is defined in section 707(c). A guaranteed minimum is an amount which the partner will receive in any case, i.e., when his share of the profits falls short of some projected level. Only the difference between the partner's share of profits (determined before any guaranteed payment) and the guaranteed minimum is considered a guaranteed payment (Rev Rul 66-95 and Reg 1.707-1(c) Example 2). Also see Rev Rul 69-180 and the other examples under Reg 1.707-1(c).

12. No deduction is allowed for losses on direct or indirect exchanges between a partnership and a person (or between 2 partnerships) where more than a 50% interest in capital or profits is owned by the transacting person (or the same persons own more than 50% of capital or profits in both partnerships).

13. No. Such loss can be offset against future gains recognized on further sales or exchanges of the same property to an unrelated party under section 267(d). [Reg 1.707-1(b)(1)(ii)]

14. The related party who acquired the property on which the loss was disallowed. [Sec 267(d)(2)]

15. The partnership is allowed the $1,000 loss, but X's distributive share is disallowed to him. [Reg 1.267(b)-1(b)]

16. Except where the asset is a capital asset in the hands of the transferee, capital gain treatment is disallowed on sales or exchanges between a partnership and a person owning more than 50% of the capital or profits, or between two partnerships in which the same persons own more than 50% of the capital or profits.

17. Section 707(c) payments are specifically excluded from section 267 treatment. This would appear to be unnecessary since section 707(c) payments must be reported for the year in which the partnership gets a deduction, hence no significant deferral could occur. The new rule will apply to section 707(a) payments, however. An accrual basis partnership will not be allowed a deduction until payments are made to a cash basis partner.

X. TRANSFERS OF PARTNERSHIP INTERESTS

1. Section 741 provides that character is capital except as provided in section 751.

2. Seller recognizes ordinary income to the extent of his share of unrealized receivables and substantially appreciated inventory.

3. Money and fair market value of property received [Sec 1001(b)] plus share of liabilities discharged [Sec 752(d)] and Reg 1.1001-2(a)(1)]. Nonrecourse liabilities are also included [Crane].

4. All section 705 adjustments up to date of sale. [Reg 1.705-1(a)]

5. Cost, determined under subchapter O. [Sec 742]

6. None, unless an election is made under section 754. [Sec 743(a)]

7. Payments are considered either as income payments under section 736(a) or as property payments under section 736(b).

8. It can usually be determined by the intent of the parties. Looking to the results will often reveal the true intent, e.g., upon liquidation, were the remaining partners' interests increased accordingly.

9. By looking to the language of any documents generated by the transaction to see whether such was described as sale, retirement, liquidation, etc. Also, by looking to the results.

10 The structure should not matter as long as the transaction reflects its true substance and receives consistent treatment among all the parties.

11. Character could be affected, i.e., sale of appreciated inventory results in ordinary gain, whereas sale of a partnership interest (where the inventory is not substantially appreciated) results in capital gain. Holding periods may differ.

12. Case history reveals that sale of a going business will usually be a sale of partnership interest(s) while discontinuation will be a sale of assets. [See McKee, paragraph 15.03]

13. No gain or loss recognized in "like-kind" exchanges. Section 1031 specifically excludes exchanges of partnership interests from like-kind treatment. The committee reports specifically state that the exclusion will not apply to exchanges of partnership interests in the same partnership. In such cases Rev. Rul. 84-52 should control.

14. Rev. Rul. 84-115 does not apply to exchanges between two parties, but rather to a contribution of a partnership interest in one partnership to the capital of another partnership. The transaction falls under section 721 and is generally tax-free.

15. If the partnership has no liabilities, then abandonment will probably result in an ordinary loss. However, if the partnership has liabilities, the release of liability will be treated as a cash distribution under section 752. This will be treated as an exchange for the partnership interest and thus be subject to "capital" treatment. [See *O'Brien v Commissioner*, 77TC 113 (1981)]

16. Yes. In *Guest v Commissioner,* 77 TC 9, the Tax Court found a gain to the extent that a nonrecourse liability exceeded basis on property contributed to a charity. A similar result is reached in Rev. Rul. 81-163, i.e., part sale and part contribution treatment.

XI. PARTNERSHIP HOT ASSETS

1. Unrealized receivables include any rights to payment for goods delivered or to be delivered, or services rendered or to be rendered. [Sec 751(c)] Note that it is the legal right to payment arising from a completed sale or contract for sale. Where a contract is only partially completed the question arises as to whether the entire contract price or only the completed portion represents the entire amount of the unrealized receivable. The better position should be to use only the completed portion, as that is most likely the only portion in which the taxpayer has enforceable rights (of course there may be exceptions, e.g., specially manufactured goods).

2. No. Only accounts receivable will be excluded since they have been realized under the accrual method of accounting. Various recapture items (e.g., sections 1245 and 1250) and installment receivables also fall under the definition of unrealized receivables.

3. Yes. Any costs not previously taken as a tax deduction. [Reg 1.751-1(c)(2)] Regulation 1.751-1(c)(5) provides that the basis of section 1245 and section 1250 recapture potential is zero.

4. Stock in trade as described in section 1221(1) and any property other than capital assets or other than section 1231 property. [Sec 751(d)(2)] Note that this definition includes receivables from the ordinary course of business as well as any unrealized receivables. [Reg 1.751-1(d)(2)(ii)]

5. When their fair market value exceeds 120% of their adjusted basis *AND* 10% of the fair market value of all assets other than money. [Sec 751(d)(1)]

6. Because of the potential abuse of trying to beat the 10% test by pumping extra cash into the partnership.

7. Convert cash to other assets or otherwise increase the amount of other assets; sell inventory for cash, or factor accounts receivable.

8. In the aggregate. [Reg 1.751-1(d)(1)]

9. It is the difference between the portion of the selling price allocated to section 751 property and the selling partner's basis in such property. [Reg 1.751-1(a)(2)]

10. Regulation 1.751-1(a)(2) provides that an arm's-length agreement between the buyer and seller will control. If there is no agreement, the selling price might be allocated in one of several different ways: the sales price could be allocated pro-rata according to fair market values of all the property in the partnership; alternatively, the selling price might be allocated first to section 751 property for its full fair market value and any remainder allocated to other property. The latter approach may be preferred where the price paid exceeds fair market value, as it will increase capital gain. Of course, the argument that the excess is attributable to goodwill is also available.

11. Regulation 1.751-1(a)(2) provides that basis is equal to the basis the partner would have had under section 732 if the property had been distributed in a current distribution.

12. (a) $42,000 ($29,500 cash + $12,500 liability release).

(b) $22,500 ($10,000 plus $12,500 in liabilities or 1/2 of the adjusted basis of partnership assets).

(c) $60,000 ($20,000 A/R, $30,000 Inventory, and $10,000 in section 1245 potential recapture).

(d)

	FMV	Basis
Accounts Receivable	$20,000	$ 0
Inventory	30,000	15,000
TOTAL	$50,000	$15,000

The inventory is substantially appreciated since the FMV exceeds basis by more than 120% and the FMV exceeds 10% of the FMV of all assets except money.

(e) $30,000 (1/2 of the total in (c) above; or alternatively $28,000 (60/90 times $42,000). See question 10 above.

(f) $7,500 (1/2 of the partnership's $15,000 basis).

(g) $22,500 ($30,000 proceeds in (e) minus $7,500 basis in (f) above); alternatively, $20,500 ($28,000 proceeds in (e) minus $7,500 basis).

	TOTAL	Sec 751	Capital
Proceeds	$42,000	$30,000	$12,000
Basis	22,500	7,500	15,000
Gain (Loss)	$19,500	$22,500	$(3,000)

ALTERNATIVELY:

	TOTAL	Sec 751	Capital
Proceeds	$42,000	$28,000	$14,000
Basis	22,500	7,500	15,000
Gain (Loss)	$19,500	$20,500	$(1,000)

XII. PARTNERSHIP DISTRIBUTIONS

1. Liquidating—one or more distributions that terminate a partner's entire interest. Current—one which is not a liquidating distribution. Regulation 1.761-1(d) specifies that where liquidating distributions are made in a series, the interest will not be considered liquidated until the final distribution is made.

2. Section 731(b) provides that generally no gain or loss is recognized by a partnership on a distribution to a partner; however, section 731(c) provides for an exception where section 751 applies.

3. Only when cash received exceeds the partner's basis in her partnership interest, but only to the extent of the excess [Sec 731(a)(1)]. Remember that liabilities assumed by the partnership will be treated as cash distributions under section 752(b).

4. Only on liquidating distributions and only where the distribution consists solely of any combination of money, unrealized receivables and inventory. [Sec 731(a)(2)]

5. The loss is equal to the excess of partnership interest basis over money plus partnership basis in unrealized receivables and inventory distributed. Example: Partner X receives a liquidating distribution of $5,000 cash, and inventory with basis of $8,000 and fair

market value of $15,000. X's basis in her partnership interest is $20,000. X recognizes a capital loss of $7,000 and has $8,000 basis in the inventory.

6. Section 731(a) specifies that gain or loss recognized is determined as if the partner sold or exchanged his partnership interest. This would require recognition of ordinary income if hot assets were held by the partnership. Note that this would direct one to section 741 which takes into account ordinary treatment on hot assets under section 751.

7. Possibly, if not considered as withdrawals of income. Income is considered earned on the last day of the partnership year. Withdrawals could be considered in excess of basis, but regulation 1.731-1(a)(1)(ii) provides that withdrawals of income are also considered as made on the last day of the partnership year.

8. The same basis that the partnership had, but such basis may not exceed the partner's basis in his partnership interest less any money received by the partner in the same transaction. [Sec 732(a)]

9. (a) None. Gain is not recognized unless cash distributed exceeds partnership interest basis. Loss is never recognized in a current distribution.
   (b) $6,000. The same as the partnership had, since this is a current distribution and the partnership basis does not exceed the partner's partnership interest basis.
   (c) $1,000: $10,000 minus the $3,000 cash and $6,000 property distributed.

10. No gain or loss is recognized. The basis of the property is limited to the remaining partnership interest basis of $7,000, $10,000 minus the $3,000 cash distribution. The partnership interest basis is zero.

11. The same basis that the partner had in his partnership interest prior to the distribution less any cash distributed in liquidation. [Sec 732(b)] Section 732(c)(1) limits the basis of inventory and unrealized receivables to the lesser of partnership interest basis or adjusted basis of such assets to the partnership.

12. Step 1: Unrealized receivables and inventory take the same basis the partnership had; but if the partner's partnership interest basis is less than the partnership basis, then the partnership basis is allocated to these items in proportion to their respective bases.

    Step 2: All other property distributed is allocated any remaining partnership interest basis in proportion to respective bases of such other property to the partnership. [Sec 732(c)]

13. Partnership interest basis is reduced by the $2,000 cash distribution, leaving a balance of $15,000. The inventory picks up the partnership's basis of $3,000. This leaves $12,000 of basis to be allocated to the other assets as follows: Capital asset—2000/6000 x $12,000 or $4,000; and depreciable asset—4000/6000 x $12,000 or $8,000. Note that any section 1245 or 1250 recapture would carry over to the partner upon the distribution; however, if he sells the depreciable asset for $6,000 his loss will be $2,000. Can he escape recognizing recapture? Service will probably say no. Here they will assert $2,000 in ordinary recapture income combined with $4,000 section 1231 loss. [But see section 1245 (b)(6).]

14. Section 735(a) will cause ordinary income to be recognized on a subsequent sale or collection of unrealized receivables and subsequent sale of inventory items within 5 years from the date the inventory was distributed.

15. Only if he does not hold the inventory in the capacity of inventory, i.e., held as investment or property used in trade or business. [Reg 1.735-1(a)(2)]

16. No, but he can for other assets. [Sec 735(b)]

17. They are considered partnership distributions in the year in which actually withdrawn. Follow the normal distribution rules. They may not be treated as withdrawals of the future income even if prepayments have been received. [Rev Rul 81-241]

XIII. DISPROPORTIONATE DISTRIBUTIONS

1. When a partner receives or relinquishes more than his proportionate share of "hot assets" in a distribution.

2. A fictional distribution to the distributee partner followed by a fictional sale and purchase between the distributee partner and the partnership.

3. Yes. Proportionate distributions, distributions to a partner who originally contributed the property, drawings, advances, gifts, and payments for services. [Sec 751(b)(2) and Reg 1.751-1(b)]

4. The character of the property relinquished. [Reg 1.751-1(b)(2)(iii)]

5. No. Regulation 1.751-1(b)(2)(ii) allocates all partnership income so recognized to the non-distributee partners.

6. Regulation 1.751-1(b)(1)(i) treats the distribution as a sale with regard to X's share of inventory retained by the partnership.

    (a) Since the transaction is treated as a distribution followed by a purchase, the partnership increases its basis in inventory by the amount of appreciation on X's share.

    (b) By subtracting X's share of partnership cash from cash received and adding the result to the amount of liabilities X is released from.

    (c) If X had received more than his proportionate share of inventory, then section 751(b) treats the transaction as a sale by the partnership of the excess inventory to X, followed by a distribution to X of his proportionate share of inventory.

7. **(a)** $4,000, the amount distributed ($7,000) less C's share ($3,000).

    (b) $4,000, the fair market value of the excess inventory received.

    (c) $3,000, which is his proportionate share of asset basis.

    (d) $2,667 ($4,000 x 6000/9000), i.e., fair market value of excess inventory, times total inventory basis divided by total inventory fair market value.

    (e) C recognizes $1,000 ($4,000 - $3,000), and the partnership recognizes $1,333 ($4,000 - $2,667).

8. The normal distribution rules under sections 731 - 736 apply. [Reg 1.751-1(b)(1)(ii)]

9. Schedule of Assets Sold and Purchased

Asset	A's Basis	FMV	Received by A	Excess over 1/3 share	Asset Value Relinquished
Cash	$5,000	$5,000	$25,000*	$20,000	$ 0
A/R	5,000	5,000	0	0	5,000
Inv.**	10,000	15,000	0	0	15,000
Land	10,000	15,000	15,000	0	0

    * Release of liability is treated as cash payment under section 752(b).

    ** Inventory, as defined in section 751(d)(2), is substantially appreciated since $60,000 is more than 120% of $45,000 and $60,000 is more than 10% of $105,000.

Since A relinquished her share of "hot assets," 751(b) is triggered. A's share of inventory and receivables is deemed distributed to her in a "current" distribution. A is then treated as selling the "hot assets" to the partnership for cash. Finally, A is then considered to have received a liquidating distribution of $5,000 cash plus $15,000 in land. The partnership is treated as having purchased A's share of "hot assets." The results are:

Tax Consequences to Partner:	
(1) Fictional distribution	
A's original basis	$30,000
Basis of inventory deemed distributed (1/3)***	(15,000)
A's remaining partnership interest basis	15,000
(2) Fictional sale	
Selling price is FMV	$20,000
Basis of inventory above***	(15,000)
A's ordinary gain	5,000
(3) Liquidating distribution	
A's adjusted basis above	$15,000
Less A's share of cash distributed	(5,000)
A's remaining partnership interest basis	10,000

$10,000 becomes A's basis in the land under 732(b).

Tax Consequences to Partnership:
The partnership has purchased A's share of accounts receivable for $5,000 and inventory for $15,000 and has a total basis of $15,000 in the receivables, $35,000 in inventory, and $20,000 in remaining land. It recognizes no gain or loss on the transaction.

*** Inventory includes accounts receivable from ordinary operations. [Reg 1.751-1(d)(2)]

10. (a)

Asset	C's Basis	FMV	Received by C	Excess Over 1/3 Share	Asset Value Relinquished
Cash	$5,000	$5,000	$22,000**	$17,000	-------
Inv*	10,000	13,000	----	----	$13,000
Prop	14,000	16,000	15,000	----	1,000***
Land	3,000	3,000	----	----	3,000
Tot	$32,000	$37,000	$37,000	$17,000	$17,000

Tax Consequences to C:

(1) Fictional Distribution
Share of section 751 assets relinquished is $13,000. C's $32,000 partnership interest basis is reduced by the $10,000 basis of the section 751 assets deemed distributed.

(2) Fictional Sale
C recognizes $3,000 ordinary income since the FMV of the section 751 assets exceeds basis by that amount.

(3) Liquidating Distribution
C's $22,000 adjusted basis remaining (after step 1) is reduced by the portion of cash not received for the sale of section 751 assets, or $9,000 ($22,000 - $13,000). According to

section 732(b) this remaining basis of $13,000 is C's basis in the depreciable property distributed.

Tax Consequences to Partnership:

The partnership recognizes no gain or loss on the transaction. It increases its basis in inventory by $3,000 ($10,000 cost of inventory purchased over $7,000 basis of inventory deemed distributed).

    * Includes accounts receivable with FMV and basis of $3,000.

   ** Includes C's liabilities of $12,000 assumed by the partnership.

 *** Logical assumption from facts in regulation is that there is no recapture.

10. (b)

Asset	C's Basis	FMV	Received by C	Excess Over 1/3 Share	Asset Value Relinquished
Cash	$5,000	$5,000	$17,000**	$12,000	----
Inv*	10,000	13,000	20,000	7,000	----
Prop	14,000	16,000	----	----	16,000
Land	3,000	3,000	----	----	3,000
Tot	$32,000	$37,000	$37,000	$19,000	$19,000

(1) Fictional Distribution

Since the facts in the regulation state that excess inventory was exchanged for depreciable property, only depreciable property is considered as distributed in this step. The fair market value of the excess inventory equals the amount of depreciable property deemed distributed; therefore, $7,000 of depreciable property is deemed distributed. The basis of such is the proportion of property deemed distributed over C's total share times C's share of partnership basis in such property, or $6,125 (7,000/16,000 x 14,000). C's partnership basis is accordingly reduced by $6,125 to $25,875.

(2) Fictional Sale

C recognizes $875 in section 1231 gain ($7,000 FMV less $6,125 basis).

(3) Liquidating Distribution

C's remaining basis of $25,875 is first reduced by the $17,000 cash received. The remaining $8,875 is assigned to the $13,000 worth of inventory distributed. C's total basis in inventory is $15,875 ($8,875 final partnership interest basis plus $7,000 in purchased inventory).

Tax Consequences to Partnership:

The partnership recognizes $2,100 ordinary income on sale of inventory with basis of $4,900 (21,000/30,000 x 7000).

The partnership increases depreciable property basis by $875 ($7,000 sale price less $6,125 basis distributed).

    * Includes accounts receivable with basis and FMV of $3000.

   ** Includes $12,000 liability assumed by partnership.

XIV. PAYMENTS TO RETIRED AND DECEASED PARTNERS

1. Section 736(a)—income payments
   Section 736(b)—property payments

2. Payments for the value of property are section 736(b) payments; any excess is a section 736(a) payment. [Reg 1.736-1(b)(5)]

3. It is "the valuation placed by the partners upon a partner's interest in partnership property in an arm's length agreement..." [Reg 1.736-1(b)(1)]

4. Section 736(a) payments, since they are not considered payments for property. [Sec 736(b)(2)(A)]

5. Capital, except for the portion of the payment for substantially appreciated inventory, which would be considered a disproportionate distribution under section 751(b).

6. It depends. If specifically provided for in the partnership agreement, they are considered property payments; if not, they are income payments. [Reg 1.736-1(b)(3)]

7. Payments for such are considered property payments to the extent of basis. [Reg 1.736-1(b)(3)]

8. (a) The following formula from regulation 1.736-1(b)(5)(i) dictates the amount.

$$\frac{\text{Fixed payment} \times \text{Total property payments}}{\text{Total payments}} = \frac{\text{Property}}{\text{Payment}}$$

(b) All payments are first section 736(b) payments to the extent of the partner's value in such assets; any excess is a section 736(a) payment. [Reg 1.736-1(b)(5)(ii)]

(c) The excess over the predetermined section 736(b) amount is considered a section 736(a) payment.

Example:

Annual fixed payment		$30,000
Total payments		$300,000
Total section 736(b) payment		$200,000

$30,000 \times \frac{200,000}{300,000} = $20,000$ annual 736(b) payment

If more than $30,000 is paid in one year all payments in excess of $20,000 are section 736(a) payments. [Reg 1.736-1(b)(5)(i)]

Question what happens if prepayments for a subsequent year are made. Under the language of the regulation it appears that in that case less than the total section 736(a) allocation will be picked up as such. Obviously such prepayments should be allocated between section 736(b) and section 736(a) payments, rather than treating the entire excess over the current year's section 736(b) payment as a section 736(b) payment. Unfortunately, there is no specific language in the regulations regarding this problem.

(d) The entire payment is a section 736(b) payment and any excess paid in subsequent year(s) is first considered a section 736(b) payment to the extent of any prior year's underpayment. [Reg 1.7361(b)(5)(i)]

9. No. The taxpayer can elect this method of reporting, but if he does not, then all basis is treated as recovered first. [Reg 1.736-1(b)(6)]

10. The year in which such payments are received. [Reg 1.736-1(a)(5)]

11. Income payments are split into two categories: section 736(a)(1), distributive share and section 736(a)(2), guaranteed payments.

12. No. Guaranteed payments are automatically ordinary, but a distributive share may include capital items or even tax-exempt income.

13. If determined with regard to income, they are considered a share of income; if not, then they are considered a guaranteed payment. [Sec 736(a)]

14. The taxable year with or within which ends the partnership taxable year for which the partnership was entitled to a deduction, or for which the payment is a distributive share. [Reg 1.736-1(a)(5)]

15. Only section 736(a)(2) payments constitute a deduction, and only for purposes of determining income under section 162(a). [Reg 1.7361(a)(4)]

XV. SPECIAL BASIS ADJUSTMENTS

1. $4,000. Section 732 provides that the basis of the property received cannot exceed the partner's partnership interest basis.

2. Yes. There is no way for the distributee partner to pick up the difference.

3. No. Since $2,000 is lost in the distribution, total partnership asset basis is now $2,000 less than total partnership interest basis.

4. No. Since $2,000 in basis was lost, any subsequent related gain (loss) would be overstated (understated) by $2,000.

5. A Sec. 754 election will allow the partnership to adjust its asset bases to reflect the $2,000 unused basis on the prior distribution.

6. Section 734(b) and related regulations when dealing with a distribution and section 743(b) and related regulations when there has been a sale of a partnership interest.

7. No. Regulation 1.754-1(a) specifies that the election applies to both sections 734(b) and 743(b).

8. No. Once made, the election is binding for all subsequent years unless revoked with permission of the district director. [Reg. 1.754-1(a)]

9. By the due date of the return for the year in which the election is being made (including extensions thereof). [Reg. 1.754-1(b)]

10. The purchaser's purchase price, i.e., cost.

11. Fair market value of the assets in the partnership.

12. Most likely, since he will usually pay more than the selling partner's share of partnership asset basis.

13. $7,500, 1/4 share of the $30,000 partnership basis.

14. $2,500, his 1/4 share of the $10,000 partnership profit.

15. No. He will be able to offset the artificial gain when the partnership liquidates his partnership interest or when he sells his entire interest. However, he will receive capital gain or loss treatment only.

16. To equalize inside and outside basis and prevent gain or loss recognition prior to the proper time.

17. It is equal to the difference between the transferee's proportionate share of asset basis and his adjusted basis in his partnership interest. [Reg. 1.743-1(b)(1)]

18. It is equal to his share of partnership capital and surplus plus his share of partnership liabilities. Section 704(c) is taken into account in making the determination. [Reg. 1.743-1(b)(1)]

19. The transferee partner only. [Reg. 1.743-1(b)(1)]

20. The distributee partner is not entitled to such. The partner who was entitled to the basis adjustment either adds it to the basis of "like-kind" property he receives in the same distribution or reallocates the basis adjustment to other "like-kind" property. [Reg. 1.743-1(b)(2)(ii)]

21. If cash is distributed to a partner in excess of his partnership interest basis, the basis increase to the partnership is equal to the gain recognized by the distributee partner. [Reg. 1.734-1(b)(1)(i)]

OR

Where the basis of property distributed to the partner exceeds his partnership interest basis, the difference is the amount of the adjustment. [Reg. 1.734-1(b)(1)(ii)]

22. If only cash, receivables, and inventory are distributed in liquidation of a partner's entire interest and a loss is recognized under section 731(a)(2), then basis decrease is equal to the amount of loss recognized. [Reg. 1.734-1(b)(2)(i)]

OR

Where a distribution in complete liquidation consists of property with a basis to the partnership which is less than the partner's partnership interest basis, the difference is the amount of the adjustment. [Reg. 1.734-1(b)(2)(ii)]

23. The partnership, i.e., all the partners. The regulations do not exclude the recipient partners in a current distribution from sharing in the basis adjustment; however, a special allocation under section 704 may be appropriate to protect all the partners.

24. If the distributee receives property in a current distribution and is unable to utilize the entire special basis adjustment, any unused portion should attach to any subsequent like-kind acquisitions of the partnership under section 755(b). If the distributee receives property in liquidation [other than that to which the section 743(b) adjustment applies], regulation 1.7342(b)(1) provides that any unused excess is carried over to the partnership. If the distributee receives property [to which the section 743(b) adjustment applies] in liquidation, it is not clear from the regulations whether or not the partnership is entitled to any unused portion. It would seem that the partnership should be entitled to any carryover under the same logic underlying regulation 1.734-2(b)(1).

25. Section 755 requires a split of the partnership assets into two categories: capital and section 1231 assets, and other assets.

26. (a) The amount is equal to the difference between the transferee's purchase price (or fair market value to the estate) and his share of basis in each class of assets. [Reg. 1.755-1(b)(2)]

(b) If the adjustment arises from a distribution resulting in a gain or loss, the adjustment is equal to the gain or loss recognized. Furthermore, the allocation may only be made to capital and section 1231 assets. [Reg. 1.755-1(b)(1)(ii)] If the adjustment arises from property distributions, the amount of the adjustment is equal to the difference between the partner's adjusted basis in his partnership interest and the partnership basis in the distributed property. Furthermore, the allocation may only be made to assets with a character similar to those assets distributed. [Reg. 1.755-1(b)(1)(i)]

27. In a manner which reduces the difference between basis and fair market value, allocated on a pro-rata basis determined by the relative appreciation or depreciation in each individual asset. [Reg. 1.755-1(a)(1)]

28. (a) No. However, under section 732(d) he can elect (or it may be mandatory) section 743(b) treatment on eligible property subsequently distributed to him.

   (b) No later than the first tax year in which such basis adjustment affects taxable income. [Reg. 1.732- 1(d)(2)(ii)]

   (c) The same as under section 743(b), except that the partnership does not make the adjustment.

29. Probably not. There is no provision for allowing carryover to the partnership.